Psychology and adult learning

Psychology and adult learning

Second edition

Mark Tennant

London and New York

First published 1997
by Routledge
11 New Fetter Lane, London EC4P 4EE

Simultaneously published in the USA and Canada
by Routledge
29 West 35th Street, New York, NY 10001

Reprinted 1999, 2000

Routledge is an imprint of the Taylor & Francis Group

© 1988 and 1997 Mark Tennant

Typeset in Palatino by
Ponting–Green Publishing Services, Chesham,
Buckinghamshire
Printed and bound in Great Britain by
Biddles Ltd, Guildford and King's Lynn

British Library Cataloguing in Publication Data
A catalogue record for this book is available from the
British Library

Library of Congress Cataloguing in Publication Data
Tennant, Mark.
    Psychology and adult learning / Mark Tennant.–2nd edn.
       p.   cm.
    Includes bibliographical references (p.   ) and index.
    1. Adulthood–Psychological aspects.   2. Adult
learning.   3. Learning, Psychology of.   4. Psychology.
I. Title.
BF724.85.C64T46   1997
155.6–dc20   96–28530

ISBN 0–415–14991–6

Contents

List of figures and tables

FIGURES

TABLES

Preface

The first edition of *Psychology and Adult Learning* was written while I was a Visiting Fellow with the Department of Continuing Education at the University of Warwick in 1986. This second edition was written while a Visiting Professor with the Center for Research and Development in Higher Education, Hokkaido University, Japan, during the northern winter of 1995–6. It has thus been ten years since I began work on the first edition. Over this decade, writes Welton (1995):

> voices from the margins of the field – armed with interpretive strategies from hermeneutical, critical and postmodernist studies – have been levelling four fundamental accusations against the modern practice of adult education: (1) adult education has abandoned its once vital role in fostering democratic social action, (2) the discipline of adult learning was based on a shaky foundation, (3) the contemporary modern practice of adult education is governed by an instrumental rationality that works to the advantage of business, industry and large scale organisations, (4) the guiding principle of the modern practice of adult education, self directed learning, is conceptually inadequate to serve the interests of the poor, oppressed, and disenfranchised in global . . . society.

He goes on to say that

> the chaos and disorder so evident in the field of adult education as discourse and practice is largely attributable to the theoretical bankruptcy of the andragogical model.

During the same period Bruner (1990) writes that the development of psychology as a discipline

> has become fragmented as never before in its history. It has lost its center and risks losing the cohesion needed to assure the internal exchange that might justify a division of labour between its parts. And the parts, each with its own organisational identity, its own theoretical apparatus, and often its own journals, have become specialities whose products become less and less exportable.

Perhaps these comments lend further weight to the postmodernist interpretation of contemporary society, that fragmentation, diversity, difference, and multiple identities are replacing cohesion, convergence,
sameness, and singular identities in our working, civic and private lives.
In spite of any misgivings voiced about the state of adult education theory,
and psychology as a foundation discipline within it, adult education as an
activity is arguably becoming more urgent and central. This is particularly
so given that demarcations between formal and nonformal educational
institutions are breaking down, new interdisciplinary groupings are being
formed which challenge the old disciplines, and formal educational
institutions no longer enjoy a monopoly on either pedagogical expertise
or the creation of knowledge. Adult education is beginning to fill some of
the spaces created by the fragmentation of the old educational systems.

In this context I believe it makes sense to continue the project of linking
psychology to issues and practices in adult education. But not for the
purpose of psychologising the process of adult learning and certainly not
to resurrect a monolithic and singular theory of adult learning. Rather the
purpose is to acknowledge the psychological dimension of adult education
work, and to explore this dimension in the context of the concerns of adult
educators, and global social and economic conditions.

It is a book about psychology and adult learning as opposed to being a
book about *the* psychology of adult learning. The reader who wants a
comprehensive account of psychology and its application to adult learning
should look elsewhere. Similarly, the reader who wants an exhaustive
treatment of any particular theory will not find it here. My approach has
been to examine the seminal traditions of some key psychological theories
and to discuss the issues and problems in applying them to an understanding of adult learning and development. I hope it will be useful for
those who seek a critical understanding of psychological theory and
research from the perspective of the adult educator.

Many of the ideas grew out of lectures and seminars delivered to
graduate students in the adult education programme at the University of
Technology, Sydney. These students were enrolled in one of a number of
courses leading to an award in adult education. They comprised community educators, industrial and commercial trainers, Aboriginal educators, ESOL (English for speakers of other languages) teachers, literacy
teachers, outreach workers, health education officers and so on. They were
all practising adult educators who had completed undergraduate studies
in psychology or a related discipline. This is the readership for whom the
book will be most accessible – the graduate student who has a knowledge
of psychology, and work experience in adult education.

I should like to express my gratitude to the following colleagues and
friends who have made direct and indirect contributions to the book:
Susan Roberts, who read the draft and made many valuable suggestions;

Chris Duke, who was my host at the University of Warwick; John Martin, who was a valuable mentor during my days at Macquarie University; my colleagues in the adult education programme at the University of Technology, Sydney; Professor Ogasawara and his colleagues for kindly inviting me to Hokkaido University; and Peter Jarvis, who stimulated me to write the book and provided valuable editorial guidance.

I am indebted to the following publishers for permission to reproduce diagrams and figures:

1 Taylor & Francis, for allowing substantial excerpts from an article published in the *International Journal of Lifelong Education* to be used in Chapter 2: M. Tennant (1986) 'An evaluation of Knowles' theory of adult learning', 5 (2): 113–22.
2 Little, Brown & Company, for Tables 4.3 and 4.6, which appear in *Adaptation to Life* by George E. Vaillant. © Copyright 1977 by George E. Vaillant.
3 Jossey-Bass, for Table 4.4, which appears in *The Modern American College* by Arthur W. Chickering (ed.) (1981).
4 Gulf Publishing, Houston, for Table 8.2, which appears in *Learning in Groups* (2nd edn) by D. Jaques (1992).
5 Croom Helm, for Table 9.1, which appears in *Adult Learning and Education* by Malcolm Tight (ed.) (1983).
6 Writers and Readers Publishing Co-operative, for Figure 9.1, which appears in *Education: The Practice of Freedom* by Paulo Freire (1974).

I would also like to thank my immediate family: Susan, Annie and Erin.

Mark Tennant
Hokkaido, Japan, February 1996

Chapter 1

Introduction

Existing approaches to understanding adult learning generally fall within one of three broad types. The first type seeks to provide a balanced overview of psychological, sociological, and philosophical theory and research together with an assessment of its relevance to adult education (e.g. Cross 1981; Long 1983; Candy 1991; Merriam and Caffarella 1991). The emphasis is generally pragmatic: a description of various aspects of psychology is developed into an eclectic understanding of how adults best learn; this may be followed by a tentative list of principles to be adopted or procedures to be employed when teaching adults. There will usually be some comments about the conceptual ambiguities of a theory or the difficulties in verifying a particular research finding, but these are often parenthetical comments, set aside from the thrust of the text. A second type of approach to understanding adult learning is one which has a clearly articulated thesis and which uses the literature to support the thesis being proposed (e.g. Tough 1979, 1982; Knowles 1984, 1990a; Mezirow 1991a; Jarvis 1992). Typically there is an attempt to identify and draw upon a selected set of psychological, sociological, and philosophical concepts and principles and thereby develop a programmatic (and sometimes prescriptive) statement about adult teaching and learning.

With respect to the psychological dimension (which is the principal concern of this book), neither of the above approaches leads to a critical understanding of the theories in question. This is understandable, because when the agenda is clearly 'adult learning' rather than 'psychology', it appears cumbersome and unnecessary to address the conceptual and methodological problems of psychological theory and research. Nevertheless, failure to do so will mean that psychology will continue to be used in an uncritical way to support the normative rhetoric of adult education.

A third approach takes as its point of departure a critical analysis of theory and research in adult education and develops from this a view about adult teaching and learning (e.g. Griffin 1983; Brookfield 1986; Hart 1990a, 1990b; Collins 1991). To date, instances of this type have typically drawn upon a range of disciplines, such as sociology, history, educational theory and, of course, psychology. My purpose in writing this book is to adopt the spirit of this approach, but to orient it towards a focus on psychology as a foundation discipline in adult education.

Jerome Bruner in his *Acts of Meaning* (1990) argues that contemporary psychology has become fragmented, that it has lost touch with the broader intellectual community, and that it needs to refocus on the great psychological questions, once again 'questions about the nature of mind and its processes, questions about how we construct our meanings and our realities, questions about the shaping of mind by history and culture' (Bruner 1990: xi). Once psychology addresses meaning as a central issue it invariably concerns itself with culture:

> A cultural psychology, almost by definition, will not be preoccupied with 'behavior' but with 'action' . . . and more specifically, with *situated action*, action situated in a cultural setting, and in the mutually inter-acting intentional states of the participants.
>
> (Bruner 1990: 19)

As such, psychology will need to ally itself once again with the interpretive disciplines in the humanities and the social sciences such as philosophy, history, linguistics, sociology and anthropology. Instead of the positivist concerns with identifying cause–effect relationships, prediction and control, and the search for universal 'culture free' aspects of the person, a cultural psychology embraces culture and the quest for meaning within culture as the key to understanding human action:

> A cultural psychology is an interpretive psychology, in much the same sense that history and anthropology and linguistics are interpretive disciplines. . . . It seeks out the rules that human beings bring to bear in creating meanings in cultural contexts. These contexts are always *contexts of practice*.
>
> (Bruner 1990: 118)

It is this view of psychology that I believe can appropriately inform adult education practice.

In the chapters which follow, I aim to provide a critical account of those psychological theories which have informed contemporary adult education theory and practice. Each theory or body of research is treated separately, in a separate chapter, using two guiding principles. First, there is an attempt to provide a balance of description, critique and comments on each theory's influence on adult education. As far as possible I have limited this process to those aspects of each theory which are pertinent to the issues and concerns of adult educators.

Second, there is an emphasis on understanding psychological development throughout the life span. The reason for this is that the very notion of 'adult education' as a separate area of inquiry implies that a distinction should be made between adults and children. Moreover, it implies that development and change is a feature of adult life and that education has a continuing role to play in the lives of all adults.

In developing a critique of each theory I have been mindful of Broughton's (1981a: 81) distinction between different types and levels of critique. In summary these are:

1 Theoretical critique – where conceptual weaknesses and internal contradictions within the theory are identified.
2 Empirical critique – where the adequacy of the theory is examined in the light of the evidence.
3 Practical critique – where the form, purpose and success of the practices promoted by the theory are assessed.
4 Ideological critique – where the sociological, historical and political origins, nature and consequences of the theory are analysed and evaluated.

An exhaustive critical analysis of a given theory would require all four levels of critique. However, in this book there is a mix of levels both within and between the chapters. The aim is not to be exhaustive, but to be selective and, for each chapter, apply only that level of critique which is relevant to adult teaching and learning.

In spite of this apparent *ad hoc* approach there is a unifying theme which persists throughout the text and which provides a framework linking the different chapters. This theme concerns the nature of the relationship between the person and the social environment.

It is useful to think of the various psychological theories addressed in the texts deriving from one of two broad perspectives: depending on whether they take the person or the social environment as their point of departure. Those theories which emphasise the primacy of the person have a tendency to explain learning and development in terms of the internal make-up of the person. Thus the person is regarded as an entity having some objective form which it is the psychologist's task to discover, describe and explain. This assumption implies that the person has an integrity or autonomous dynamic which makes it largely independent of the social environment In contrast, theories which emphasise the primacy of the social environment have a tendency to explain learning and development in terms of the external forces impinging on the person. On this account the person is reduced to the dependent position, implying that the person can be explained and understood as a product of social influences, at least in all important respects.

This of course is an over-simplification and most theories admit both internal and external influences on learning and development. But nevertheless, an emphasis on one or the other term of the 'person–social environment' relation is nearly always apparent. Within the person perspective there is a tradition of research which focuses on emotional development. In this tradition, the emphasis is on how our concept of self, and the conflicts within it, emerges and develops as we proceed through the life course. The groundwork in this tradition can be traced to the humanistic psychology of Rogers and Maslow (Chapter 2), or to the psychoanalytic theory of Freud and its subsequent developments (Chapter 3). Many of the later theories of adult psychological development borrow from both the psychoanalytic and humanistic traditions (e.g. Loevinger, Gould, Levinson, Vaillant, Neugarten and Lowenthal). Adult educators have shown considerable interest in this research (e.g. see Merriam and Caffarella 1991), mainly because it offers the prospect of providing a theoretical and research base for adult teaching and learning (Chapter 4). In particular, it provides us with a model of the end point of development, the 'fully functioning person' – the autonomous, independent and integrated adult personality – from which is derived a view about how adults learn best at various stages and phases of the life cycle (see Weathersby 1981; Merriam and Clark 1991; Tennant and Pogson 1995). The other tradition within the person perspective is concerned with the person's knowledge and cognitive capacities. One area in this research attempts to explain the processes through which, in the course of our development, we attain an understanding of the world. The principal theorists and researchers in this area have been influenced by the seminal work of Piaget in the domain of cognitive development, and Kohlberg in the field of moral development. They have in common the mission of describing and explaining the sequence of stages which mark our progressive understanding of abstract concepts and moral regulations. Adult educators are interested in the extent to which we can talk of 'adult' cognitive stages, and whether the processes of stage progression are relevant to the processes of adult learning. But increasingly there is interest in work which documents intellectual capacity over the life span and/or how intelligence in adult life needs to be reconceived (Chapter 5). Other research efforts have focused on mapping individual differences in cognitive styles (Chapter 6).

The 'social environment' perspective encompasses a diverse range of theories and approaches. One class of approaches postulates a mechanistic relationship between the person and the social forces acting on it. On this account the person is a passive receiver of behaviours, roles, attitudes and values which are shaped and maintained by the social environment through rewards and sanctions. The most influential of these approaches is Skinner's stimulus–response psychology (behaviourism). His theory has had an impact on teaching and learning in all sectors of education. In adult education his legacy is most apparent in the importance attached by many adult educators to the need for setting behavioural objectives and providing regular feedback and reinforcement (Chapter 7). This mechanistic approach is also apparent in some of the descriptive research on adult life phases (e.g. Chickering and Havighurst 1981).

An opposing class of approaches within the 'social environment' perspective postulates a more active role for the person in the person–society dialectic. Learning and development are thus seen as proceeding through a constant interaction between the developing person and the social environment. Both the developing person and the social environment are active in this process – this is why it is referred to as a dialectical process. In adult education this general approach is recognisable in the writings of Freire, Lovett, Griffin, Brookfield, Mezirow and others who draw attention to the working of social processes in shaping individual identity and the need for adult learners to resist forms of enculturation which are alienating and oppressive (Chapter 9).

The above distinctions are useful as a framework for locating different psychological theories – but they are more than this. In everyday life people adopt strong views on the relationship between person and society, and those views influence their perception of political, economic and moral issues. Let me illustrate this with some examples of an extreme person perspective, which is commonly manifested in the way people attribute to individuals the responsibility for events and actions which are more properly considered social phenomena. Thus we hear that the unemployed are lazy or inept (and could therefore enter employment if they changed their attitude or improved themselves), migrants are reprehensible for failing to learn their adopted country's language and the illiterate have only themselves to blame for their incomplete schooling (and should therefore pay fees as adult second-chance learners). A variant of this tendency to attribute to the individual more responsibility and control than is warranted, is the tendency to overemphasise the natural (biological) and unalterable aspects of the individual. Thus boys are seen as naturally different from girls (and by implication attempts to change this are futile); homosexuality is deemed to be unnatural (and therefore consensus cannot establish it as a legitimate lifestyle); and it is said that there are natural racial differences in intelligence (a view which challenges the efficacy of educational intervention). These few examples, which illustrate a bias in allocating responsibility towards the individual, constitute a challenge to the wisdom or morality of collective responsibility and social intervention.

Any attempt to develop a theory of andragogy will necessarily be based on a view of the relationship between person and society; and those educators who propose educational reforms, new educational programmes, or new teaching practices, will invariably be called upon to articulate their views. This is because education as an activity explicitly links the individual with the social. In particular, adult education is seen as a vehicle for explicitly addressing significant social issues connected to areas such as the environment, race, health, gender, class, aged people, unemployed people, and the dislocation and exploitation of migrants. In the text which follows I consider in more detail the above general scenario. I argue that many of the prevailing theories in psychology and adult education lead to an over-regular and over-systematic view of adult learning and development, which is best understood as a dialectical process subject to the vagaries of historical and social variation.

Chapter 2

Humanistic psychology and the self-directed learner

Self-directed learning is one of those foundation concepts in adult education which strengthen the identity as a distinct field of practice and inquiry. The term is constantly used in journals, monographs and texts in adult education and has featured in a number of national and international policy documents. It evokes associations with a cluster of terms such as 'learner-centredness', 'independent learning', 'self-teaching', 'autonomy', 'freedom' and 'needs-meeting', all of which are enthusiastically embraced within the emerging ethos of adult education.

Like most foundation concepts, 'self-directed learning' is articulated in a way which allows seemingly limitless interpretations of what it is and how it should be applied. Stephen Brookfield has for many years provided a thoughtful analysis of the concept. In an early series of articles (1981, 1985a, 1985b, 1985c), he locates the origin of self-directed learning in three distinct schools of thought.

> To the banner of self-directed learning can be rallied those philosophers who advocate the development in students of powers of critical insight, independent thought and reflective analysis. Hence, the injunctions of Paterson and Lawson regarding the importance of using a liberal arts curriculum or of emphasising in the teaching of craft skills the cognitive, rational and intellectual dimensions, are perfectly consistent with an interpretation of a self-directed learner as an individual skilled in making judgements of the intellectual merit of various theories, arguments or propositions. Humanistically inclined adult educators can also claim philosophical kinship with the idea since it appears to be but an educational interpretation of the notion of self-actualisation. Indeed, adult educators such as Knowles and Tough, both of whom can be placed within the tradition of humanistic psychology, are the writers most associated with this concept. Finally, critical theorists of adult education such as Freire and Mezirow can also lay claim to the concept as one which neatly summarises the idea that adult education should be concerned to bring into the learner's critical consciousness those

assumptions, beliefs and values which have been uncritically assimilated and internalised during childhood and adolescence.

(Brookfield 1985a: 19)

The first of these schools of thought, the 'cultivation of the intellect'
approach, stresses the development of rational minds through a teacher-
centred and subject-focused curriculum. In this approach the self-directed
learner is considered the ideal product of a very traditional educational
experience. As such, it is an approach which is inimical to mainstream
adult education theory and practice. The remaining two schools of
thought, the 'humanistic' and the 'critical awareness', have had a profound
impact on the struggle to define the goals, purposes and practices of adult
education. In particular they have competing views concerning the nature,
rationale and purposes of self-directed learning.

In a more recent commentary on self-directed learning, Caffarella (1993)
points to three distinct ideas in the literature on self-directed learning:

a self initiated process of learning that stresses the ability of individuals
to plan and manage their own learning, an attribute or characteristic of
learners with personal autonomy as its hallmark, and a way of organ-
izing instruction in formal settings that allows for greater learner
control.

(Caffarella 1993: 25)

She points out that in addition to humanistic philosophy the concept has
been influenced by progressivism (the focus on the experience of the
learner), behaviourism (the focus on learning contracts and objectives: see
Hiemstra and Sisco 1990) and critical theory (the focus on critical reflection
and the analysis of the assumptions which guide our actions: see Mezirow
1985; Brookfield 1986; Hammond and Collins 1991; Garrison 1992).

Pursuing the same project of clarifying the nature of autonomy and self-
direction, Candy (1991) distinguishes between autonomy as a learner (to
be self-directed in learning) and autonomy as a general personal attribute.
He argues that the term self-direction refers to four distinct phenomena:
personal autonomy, the ability to manage one's own learning, a teaching
and learning environment which encourages learner control, and the
independent pursuit of learning outside formal institutions. He recognises
that self-direction can be considered a process (where learners gradually
take control of their learning) or as an ideal end point where self-direction
in a wider sense is developed, where freedom and self-determination are
the general state of affairs for a group or section of society.

Self-directed learning as a practical and theoretical concept is still
strongly linked to the work of Knowles and his model of the lifelong
learner, who possesses the following skills:

The ability to develop and be in touch with curiosities (to engage in
divergent thinking).

The ability to formulate questions ... that are answerable through inquiry (to engage in convergent or inductive–deductive reasoning).

The ability to identify the data required to answer the various kinds of questions.

The ability to locate the most relevant and reliable sources of data.

The ability to select and use the most efficient means for collecting the required data from the appropriate sources.

The ability to organize, analyze and evaluate the data so as to get valid answers.

The ability to generalize, apply and communicate the answers to the questions raised.

(Knowles 1980: 267)

The adult educator has a responsibility to foster these skills, and the best way to do this, argues Knowles, is to adopt an andragogical approach to learning. The andragogical approach is characterised by a set of assumptions that the adult teacher has about the adult learner:

1 Adults need to know why they need to learn something before commencing their learning.
2 Adults have a psychological need to be treated by others as capable of self-direction.
3 Adults have accumulated experiences and these can be a rich resource for learning.
4 In children, readiness to learn is a function of biological development and academic pressure. In adults, readiness to learn is a function of the need to perform social roles.
5 Children have a (conditioned) subject-centred orientation to learning, whereas adults have a problem-centred orientation to learning.
6 For adults the more potent motivators are internal.

(Knowles 1989: 83–4)

Using these assumptions as a starting point, Knowles proceeds to specify the skills, processes and techniques of helping adults learn. A key element in this is the learning contract, which is a device used by learners to guide and plan their learning. Typically, a learning contract requires some kind of diagnosis of needs, followed by a specification of goals and objectives, the identification of learning strategies and resources, and the evaluation of progress. In most applications of the learning contract method, the contract is negotiated between the learner and an adviser, who normally has a vested interest in the learning activities in the contract (e.g. supervisor, peer, academic).

This scenario for adult learning has been critically analysed by several commentators (Tennant 1986; Griffin 1987; Brookfield 1991; Jarvis 1992) who have highlighted the gaps between theory and practice, the untenable nature of the andragogical assumptions, the lack of supporting evidence, its conceptual limitations, and its ideological impact. The remainder of this chapter expands some of these claims.

The view that adults are, or should be, self-directed learners, receives its support from three distinct sources:

1 Empirical work on the prevalence and nature of self-directed learning.
2 The influence of humanistic clinical psychology.
3 Theoretical and empirical work in the psychology of life span development.

EMPIRICAL STUDIES

The best known and earliest empirical work on the nature and ubiquity of self-directed learning is to be found in Tough's (1967, 1968, 1979, 1982) investigations of the learning 'projects' of adults. A learning project is a major learning effort which is a deliberate and sustained (minimum 7 hours) attempt to gain some clear knowledge and skill. Using these criteria, Tough was able to show that the typical adult spends about 90–100 hours on each learning project, conducts eight such projects every year and plans or directs the projects personally. The key elements in self-directed learning are portrayed as

1 knowledge and ability to apply the basic process of planning, conducing, and evaluating learning activities
2 ability to identify one's own learning objectives
3 ability to select the appropriate planning strategy and planner expertise
4 ability to direct one's own planning when that course of action is appropriate
5 ability to make sound decisions about the setting and time management of learning activities
6 ability to gain knowledge or skill from the resources utilised
7 ability to detect and cope with personal and situational blocks to learning
8 ability to renew motivation.

The elements identified here are certainly compatible with the skills of self-directed learning identified by Knowles (1980), which were quoted earlier. In both accounts the self-directed learner is one who masters a range of learning techniques and processes. It should be noted that in addition to Tough there are studies which show that the learning process of adults is not so well planned or linear (see Spear and Mocker 1984; Danis and

Tremblay 1987; Candy 1991). The process is more haphazard and based more on trial and error than Tough's learning projects would have us believe.

Another significant development in the empirical investigation of self-directed learning has been the construction of a diagnostic text, the Self Directed Learning Readiness Scale (SDLRS: Guglielmino and Guglielmino 1982). This scale had the endorsement of a number of prominent adult educators in North America, including Chickering, Houle, Knowles and Tough. Thus the items it contains can be considered representative of the orthodox North American view of self-directed learning, at least at the time of its development.

It was Brookfield (1985c) who first pinpointed the weaknesses of this research. He argued that the structured interview schedules and prompt sheets of Tough and the measurement scale of the Guglielminos were inadequate in a number of important respects. First, the people surveyed have been primarily drawn from middle-class, educationally advantaged populations and thus Brookfield remarks

> to talk of the adults' (in a generic sense) propensity for self-directed learning on the basis of research into samples comprised chiefly of middle-class Americans is a dangerous act of intellectual ethnocentrism. Very few researchers have chosen to investigate the self-directed learning activities of working-class adults. . . .Conspicuous by their absence are studies of self-directed learning among Blacks, Puerto-Ricans, Hispanics, Asians or American Indians.
>
> (Brookfield 1985c: 24)

A second point of criticism concerns the way in which expectations play a role in influencing an interviewee's recall of a learning experience. For example, the finding by Tough, that learning projects often originate in an action goal, may be attributed to the skills-oriented examples the interviewers use when explaining the 'typical' learning project. Third, the use of questionnaires and scales presupposes a familiarity with this form of data gathering, a familiarity which cannot be assumed for all groups in society. Finally, argues Brookfield, there was insufficient attention given to the quality and worth (value) of the learning activities reported. It is also instructive to note the culture-specific nature of the Guglielmino items make no reference to group learning and appear biased towards print material and middle-class lifestyles (e.g. libraries, personal responsibility for learning, long-term goals). Since Brookfield's article there has been considerable debate about the validity and reliability of the SDLRS (Field 1989, 1991; Guglielmino et al. 1989; Candy 1991). The scale has since been renamed the Learning Preference Assessment, which is an equivalent form of the SDLRS (Guglielmino and Guglielmino 1991); a recent study strongly supports its validity (Delahaye and Smith 1995). Nevertheless, one should be cautious about claiming that adults in the community are largely self-directed learners – and that adult educators should adapt to this reality by adjusting their pedagogic practices and the nature of the service they offer.

HUMANISTIC CLINICAL PSYCHOLOGY

The influence of humanistic psychology can be seen in Knowles' conception of self-directed learning, particularly in his endorsement of the term 'self-actualisation' and in his construction of the ideal teacher–learner relationship.

The concern with the 'self' is a hallmark of humanistic psychology, which emerged as a protest against the scientific explanation of the person. Scientific methods reduce the person to the status of being an 'object' for scientific inquiry. By contrast, humanistic psychology reaffirmed the human qualities of the person – such as personal freedom, choice and the validity of subjective experience. Among the self theorists in psychology perhaps the most prominent names are Kurt Goldstein (1939), Carl Rogers (1951), Gordon Allport (1961) and Abraham Maslow (1968a). Maslow's work has had a considerable range of application and so I will take his view of self-actualisation as the paradigm. He presents his view as a theory of motivation.

In outline his theory is simple: he offers a number of categories of motive which are related in a hierarchy of prepotency. By this it is meant that the person remains under the control of the motive at the 'lower' level until the object of that motive is achieved or its satisfaction assured. As soon as this occurs the person comes under the sway of the motive force at the next (higher) level. When and only when this is satisfied the person becomes subject to the next, and so on. A motive of a lower level is always prepotent over one at a higher level. The highest, which comes into operation only when all other forces are quiescent, is called the 'need for self-actualistion'. The details of the hierarchy are as follows:

Level 1   *Physiological needs* such as hunger, thirst and sex, sleep, relaxation and bodily integrity. These must be satisfied before there come into play . . .
Level 2   *Safety needs* which call for a predictable and orderly world, safe, reliable, just and consistent. While these are not satisfied the person will be occupied in attempts to organise his/her world so as to provide the greatest possible degree of safety and security. If satisfied, he/she comes under the forces of . . .
Level 3   *Love and belongingness needs* which cause him/her to seek warm and friendly human relationships.
Level 4   *Self-esteem needs* – the desire for strength, achievement, ad-

equacy, mastery and competence, for confidence in the face of the world, independence and freedom, reputation and prestige.

Level 5 *Self-actualisation* – the full use and exploitation of talents, capacities and potentialities. Self-actualisers are able to submit to social regulation without losing their own integrity or personal independence; that is, they may follow a social norm without their horizons being bounded in the sense that they fail to see or consider other possibilities. They may on occasion transcend the socially prescribed ways of acting. Achieving this level may mean developing to the full stature of which they are capable.

The way that Maslow specifies the relationships between levels in the hierarchy exposes him to some forceful criticisms. The first concerns the claim that if one has satisfied lower needs (and not otherwise) one will necessarily proceed to the higher steps on the latter. By deduction, those who have had their every physiological and safety need satisfied throughout life will inevitably become those who develop their highest potentialities. Those who have suffered long continued deprivation of physiological and safety needs will have had little opportunity to develop their higher levels. In plain words, those raised in relative luxury will become more creative, original and integrated personalities, those raised in disadvantageous circumstances will end up as inferior products. Facts do not seem to bear this out and exceptions come too readily to mind. It is patently untrue that one must attend to the lower levels before the higher. Fugitives are not compelled to defer further attempts to evade their enemies until they have satisfied their need for food, not even if they are at the point of starvation. One is not compelled to attend to safety needs before pursuing love and belongingness. Danger often brings out strong propensities for loving, as in times of war or pestilence. Martyrs have pursued what can only be called self-actualisation under the certainty of death.

In addition to these objections concerning the relationship between levels in the hierarchy, there are some shortcomings in the way Maslow has conceptualised Level 5 in the hierarchy, self-actualisation.

It appears that to be 'self-actualised' is to be psychologically healthy, to make full use of one's talents, capacities and potentialities. It is a 'need' or 'direction' the person strives towards to achieve psychological growth. In Maslow's words, once we have achieved a certain level of maturity we are motivated primarily by trends to

> self-actualisation (defined as on-going actualisation of potentials, capacities and talents, as fulfilment of a mission (or call, fate, destiny or vocation), as a fuller knowledge of, and acceptance of, the person's own intrinsic nature, as an unceasing trend towards unity, integration or synergy within the person).
>
> (Maslow 1968a: 25)

Self-actualisers are said to have a 'superior perception of reality'; 'increased acceptance of self, or others and of nature'; an increase in 'problem-centring'; increased 'autonomy'; a greater 'freshness of appreciation' and 'richness of emotional reaction'; and a host of other qualities. The complete picture of the self-actualised person remains elusive; nevertheless, it is something, we are told, towards which we are propelled. This tendency is not under deliberate, conscious control; rather it is a constituent part of our physiological endowment; it is something which characterises us as uniquely human. What Maslow would appear to be saying, then, is that humans are 'set' to self-actualise by virtue of their physiological make-up just as a sunflower seed is 'set' by its make-up to grow into a plant and produce a flower. Environmental conditions will make a difference to the result but the person is basically a persistent developer of its potential.

Knowles adopts this view of psychological growth in his attempt to construct a model for helping adults to learn:

> the problem is that the culture does not nurture the development of the abilities required for self-direction, while the need to be increasingly self-directing continues to develop *organically*. The result is a growing gap between the need and ability to be self-directing.
>
> (Knowles 1990a: 55)

The practices that Knowles advocates are designed to narrow this gap so that the learning processes of adults are congruent with their need for psychological growth.

The main difficulty with Knowles' andragogical model (and its corollary, the learning contract) is that it can be interpreted in a number of ways: as an initial guide to assist adult learners towards self-direction; as a process of learning appropriate for adults who have already attained the capacity to be self-directed, or as a means through which individual needs can be reconciled with institutional or organisational demands. The first interpretation requires the assumption that adults are, in fact, *not* self-directing and that they need to be weaned away from traditional educational consumption. Those who subscribe to this view caution us against the too abrupt introduction of self-directed learning; they argue that this type of learning should be the goal of adult education rather than its starting point. Not surprisingly the reasons for a stance such as this may be quite disparate, ranging from a paternalistic and manipulative attitude to adult learners, through to a genuine concern with providing supports for self-directed learning efforts. Knowles certainly acknowledges the importance of building a bridge towards self-direction: 'adult educators have been devising strategies for helping adults make the transition from being dependent learners to being self-directed learners' (1984: 9) and he advises that the andragogical model should be applied selectively, as the situation permits, but this interpretation is at odds with the thrust of his thinking.

The second interpretation assumes that self-directed learners have the capacity to control and plan the content and processes through which they learn. Ironically though, while adult educators are admonished by Knowles for structuring the *content* of a course, they are praised and given guidance for structuring the *processes* to be followed in a course. But why should self-directed learners follow the *processes* advocated by Knowles? Surely the imposition of a process can be just as restrictive and alienating as the imposition of content? Many adult students report being alienated by pre-structured self-assessment forms, particularly the 'objective' check-list variety. Also, the formal learning contract, particularly when it requires the specification of behavioural objectives, can often hinder rather than assist learning.

Knowles seems to regard the learning contract *process* as somehow neutral; he thus fails to acknowledge that it contains assumptions about the nature of knowledge and knowing; and consequently these assumptions remain unexplored by him. At best, he offers a truncated version of self-direction: the student directs the *content*, the educator directs the *process*.

The third interpretation above, that the learning contract is a means of reconciling individual needs with organisation goals, is another illustration of Knowles' diminished self-directed learner. It is unreasonable to expect individual needs, at all times, to be in harmony with organisational goals, and in instances of conflict individual needs may well be compromised. This prospect raises a still more fundamental question, is the learning contract a tool for learning or a tool for educators, trainers and managers? In a revealing section of *The Adult Learner: A Neglected Species*, Knowles advocates a pragmatic approach towards the use of learning theories by trainers and adult educators. Following a description of a range of learning theories, he outlines a number of criteria we should apply before selecting one theory over another. These criteria include 'how does the proposed theory fit your organisation's management philosophy?' (Knowles 1990b: 100) and 'Another thing to check before choosing a single theory is its congruence with the organisation's long-range development goals' (1990b: 112). Thus Knowles' attitude towards the different learning theories is based on the view that they are merely 'products' to be consumed and disposed of at will. This is a questionable view because it takes no account of the explanatory force of the theories concerned.

The organisation looms large in Knowles' (1984) *Andragogy in Action*; testimony to this is the following orientation address for new employees at Lloyds Bank of California:

> You are entering an adult learning environment. This is a very participative process. We realise that you are interested in a career rather

than just a job. We will help you become aware of the skills and knowledge you will need on your growth path with us. We will expect you to participate in certain training at each step.... We will expect you to use your training as an opportunity and gain from it the information you need for your own competence and future career growth. Your test will be on the job. If you are able to carry out your functions competently as a result of training, then your manager will recognise this and consider it in growth appraisals. If you fail to take advantage of the resources offered, then you will not become competent, not progress and probably not be with us in the future.

(cited in Knowles 1984: 75)

Is this an example of 'mutual respect', 'collaborativeness', 'mutual trust', 'supportiveness', 'pleasure', 'humanness', 'mutual planning' and 'needs diagnosis' that Knowles refers to earlier in this volume?

Knowles' model for the ideal teacher–learner relationship strongly reflects the counsellor–client relationship in humanistic clinical psychology. Both Rogers and Maslow were clinical psychologists who normally dealt with individual clients, and who were concerned with the psychological health of these clients. It is not surprising, then, to find that the educational practices they advocate mirror their clinical or therapeutic techniques. This is well illustrated by Rogers' conception of the teacher as a facilitator of learning. The qualities of a good facilitator include:

1 *Realness and genuineness*

> When the facilitator is a real person, being what she is, entering into a relationship with the learner without presenting a front or facade, she is much more likely to be effective.... It means that she is being herself, not denying herself.
>
> (Rogers 1983: 122–3)

2 *Prizing, acceptance and trust*

> Think of it as prizing the learner, prizing her feelings, her opinions, her person. It is a caring for the learner. But a non-possessive caring. It is an acceptance of this other individual as a separate person, having worth in her own right. It is a basic trust – a belief that this other person is somehow fundamentally trustworthy.
>
> (Rogers 1983: 124)

3 *Empathic understanding*

> The ability to understand the student's reactions from the inside ... a sensitive awareness of the way the process of education and learning seems to the student.
>
> (Rogers 1983: 129)

The emphasis on the personal relationship between the facilitator and the learner is a feature of Knowles' conception of the andragogical teacher who 'accepts each student as a person of worth and respects his feelings and ideas . . . seeks to build relationships of mutual trust [and] exposes his own feelings' (1990b: 85–6). This is not the complete picture, and Knowles adds to these qualities other 'principles of teaching' which build on this relationship and encourage the learner to diagnose needs, set objectives, enter contractual arrangements and evaluate outcomes. It is interesting that these additional principles of andragogical teaching are similar to the strategies adopted by those psychologists who seek to encourage behaviour modification through self-direction. The use of 'well defined objectives', 'contractual agreements' and 'objective records of behavioural changes' are all seen as essential to a successful programme of behavioural change (see Bandura 1969, and a summary in Knowles 1990b: 129–33).

It appears that Knowles' andragogical teacher has been constructed from the techniques and practices of psychologists working in two quite different and opposing therapeutic traditions (the humanistic and behavioural traditions). The learning model which emerges leads to an unpalatable view of education as the identification and elimination of deficits or 'gaps' in knowledge, performance, or self-concept. For example, one principle of andragogical teaching cited by Knowles is 'The teacher helps the students identify the life problems they experience because of the gaps in their personal equipment'. Statements such as these locate the source of 'life problems' away from the institution and towards the individual with the 'solutions' being firmly implanted in the teacher–taught relationship.

A second problem with the deficit model of education relates to the diagnosis of 'deficit'; Knowles makes it clear that deficits (and therefore needs) are diagnosed not only by the learner, but also by interests external to the learner:

> the teacher involved the students in a mutual process of formulating learning objectives in which the needs of the students, of the institution, of the teacher, of the subject matter and of the society are taken into account.
>
> (Knowles 1990b: 86)

But what should the teacher do when there is a conflict of interests? Clearly the conflict will be resolved according to the distribution of power and status among the various interests and the students can be expected to fare poorly indeed. In this way the idea of 'diagnosing needs' will become yet another mechanism for legitimising existing conceptions of worthwhile education.

One final point concerns the emphasis on maintaining goodwill with the client (in therapy) or learner (in teaching). In general, this is desirable, but if goodwill means that conflict is suppressed or avoided, then it may not always be desirable. One reason for this is that conflict may well stimulate and assist learning, and this view can be supported both theoretically (Piaget 1978) and empirically (Mugny and Doise 1978). Another reason for avoiding the emphasis on goodwill is that it tends to become mandatory for both the adult teacher (as an andragogue) and the adult learner (as an andragogee). The effect of this on group behaviour is that conflict is suppressed much more and for longer than would normally be the case and the result can be catastrophic. The point being made is that a preoccupation with goodwill (i.e. goodwill = good teacher = good student) can do more harm than good; and that conflict should be seen as a natural and desirable outcome of the interaction of two or more inquiring and challenging minds.

ASSESSING THE CONTRIBUTION OF SELF-DIRECTED LEARNING AND ANDRAGOGY

Pratt (1993) frames three questions in his assessment of andragogy 'after twenty-five years': do we know more about learning? Do we know more about the antecedents of adult learning? How can we facilitate adult learning? Of course the collective contributions to the 'andragogy' literature offer responses to these questions, but whether these responses simply state a position or add to knowledge is a moot point. With respect to learning, Pratt identifies two implicit principles: first, that knowledge is actively constructed by the learner; and second, that learning is 'an interactive process of interpretation, integration, and transformation of one's experiential world' (Pratt 1993: 17). With respect to the antecedents to learning there is the individual self with a self-concept and needs, there is the assumption that the self strives for improvement and autonomy, and there is an emphasis on the uniqueness of the self and the recognition of individual differences. With respect to the facilitation of adult learning there are the well-known elements of the 'andragogical process' such as 'climate setting', and involving learners in mutual planning, diagnosis of needs, formulation of objectives, designing of learning plans, and mutual evaluation. As Pratt observes, the contribution of andragogy 'is not as grand in substance as it is in scale... it has done little to expand or clarify our understanding of the process of learning'. That the scale of its influence outstretches its substance is perhaps explained by the observation that andragogy is not really a theory of adult learning at all, it is more a philosophical position on the aims of adult education and the relationship between the person and society, a position which ultimately places faith in the potency of the individual to transcend their social and historical situation.

It is fair to say that this ethic has informed much of the adult education literature. But there is a growing opposition to this view. For example, even the very notion of autonomy and self-directed learning has been challenged by authors such as Belenky *et al.* (1986), Shrewsbury (1987), Boucouvalas (1988), Hayes (1989) and Caffarella (1993) who stress the importance of interconnectedness and interdependence as qualities reflecting women's ways of connecting with the world.

But in rejecting the individualism of self-directed, autonomous learning it is important to avoid portraying the individual as solely the product of distorting ideologies and oppressive social structures. While it is true that a purely humanistic view of the person is naive in its failure to acknowledge the power of social forces, a view of the person as totally determined is too pessimistic and leaves no scope for individual agency and autonomy. Usher (1992) offers us a third perspective: to view our experiences as texts into which our self has been inscribed and to explore alternative readings of that text. In this way we can reconstitute ourselves. This does not mean we can create any self we choose; the reading we give to our experience must be plausible and be able to legitimately contest alternative readings. In this way the autonomous self is aware of its 'situatedness' and the limits and possibilities for self-transformation.

Brookfield (1993b) too is conscious of the need to reassert the political dimensions of self-direction. Drawing on the work of Griffin (1983, 1987) and Collins (1991) he recognises that humanistic adult education has been too accommodative and depoliticised and placed too much faith in the agency of the individual. But he denies that the concepts of autonomy and self-direction are necessarily accommodative and depoliticised and argues that genuine self-directed learning fundamentally challenges institutional decision-making processes and power structures:

> The self in a self directed learning project is not an autonomous, innocent self, contentedly floating free from cultural influences. It has not sprung fully formed out of a political vacuum. It is, rather, an embedded self, a self whose instincts, values, needs and beliefs have been shaped by the surrounding culture. As such, it is a self that reflects the constraints and contradictions, as well as the liberatory possibilities, of that culture.
>
> (Brookfield 1993b: 236)

Brookfield, like Usher, sees the self as embedded or situated in history and culture, but that autonomy is possible because of the conflicts, contradictions and ambiguities of our historical and cultural situation. The key to autonomy and self-direction, then, lies in the exploration of alternative readings of our personal biographies in their historical and cultural context.

In this chapter I have argued that the rationale and empirical support for the humanistic concepts of self-development and self-direction has gaps and weaknesses which need to be acknowledged. There is a need to distinguish the rhetoric of adult education from its rationale and empirical base. The prevailing rhetoric asserts that in everyday life adults are basically self-directed and that this self-direction is rooted in our constitutional make-up; it also asserts that self-development is an inexorable process towards higher levels of existence, and finally it asserts that adult learning is fundamentally (and necessarily) different from child learning. These assertions should not be accepted as articles of faith.

Chapter 3

The psychoanalytic approach

The work of Freud has had an overwhelming impact on the development of twentieth-century social science. Its legacy is evident in contemporary psychology, sociology, anthropology, linguistics, literature, the arts, film and education. Its legacy is more than historical, and familiarity with the issues, methods and substantive content of Freudian psychoanalysis is indispensable for anyone with an interest in elucidating the human mind. Freud provides us with a language for understanding the person in everyday life, a language which is based on a total conception of the person and not some compartmentalised version of it. Perhaps this accounts for his appeal to both the academic and popular imagination.

Freud's writing is very accessible in the sense that his style is exceptional and his ideas unfold in a natural fashion (he received the Goethe Prize for literature in 1930) but, paradoxically, the totality of his thought is extremely elusive. Reasons for this are easy to find: the sheer volume of his published material, the evolution of his thought over a span of fifty years and the fact that he did not have a consistent position. All this makes it very difficult to provide a systematic account of Freud's work, let alone a thorough critique. Short textbook accounts invariably do an injustice to the complexities of psychoanalysis and they risk confirming incorrect hearsay knowledge about the subject (for example, that all little boys want to have sex with their mothers, or that we are all motivated by sex only).

Freud himself tried on a number of occasions to set out his theories systematically, notably in the publications *Introductory Lectures on Psychoanalysis*, *New Introductory Lectures on Psychoanalysis* and *An Outline of Psychoanalysis* (Freud 1973a, 1973b, 1949). But even these are incomplete because they lack the detailed, rich observations present in many of his other publications. Freud has been criticised from every conceivable angle; there are claims that his theory is the product of a neurotic, distorted mind; that its status as a science is questionable; that he was unable to free himself from the cultural milieu of his time (particularly in his views on female identity); that because his work is largely based on psychopathology, generalisations to the normal population do not hold; and that his psychotherapeutic technique simply does not work. For the most part the debate on these, and other closely allied issues, remains unresolved.

Psychoanalysis is notably absent from the literature on adult teaching and learning. This is difficult to understand, especially given the importance that adult educators attach to the emotional climate of the classroom and the anxieties, fears and hopes of learners. Indeed, there are several ways in which adult educators can profitably approach Freudian psychoanalysis:

1   As a source of clinical insight into the relationships among learners and between teachers and learners.
2   As a forceful theory which links individual identity with the way in which society is organised.
3   As a reference point for understanding psychoanalytic approaches to adult development.

CLINICAL INSIGHT AND ADULT LEARNING

Freud felt compelled to assume the existence of the unconscious. He did so for a number of reasons, which can best be understood in the context of his experiences as a physician in Vienna in the late nineteenth century. Freud became a close professional associate of Joseph Breuer who had a patient (Anna O) who exhibited the classical symptoms of hysteria. These included physical malfunctions such as partial paralysis, vomiting, disturbances of sight and speech which could not be traced to organic causes, in addition to a host of other symptoms such as confusion, feelings of helplessness and perceived worthlessness. The medical profession at the time found it difficult to know how to treat such cases. One commonly applied treatment entailed the use of hypnosis. As a phenomenon, hypnosis had attracted Freud. He had studied with Charcot and others for a brief time in Paris and was impressed with their demonstrations. Two hypnotic phenomena were particularly salient for Freud, these were post-hypnotic suggestion and the apparent ability of people to recapture, under hypnosis, otherwise forgotten memories. Later he wrote about post-hypnotic suggestion:

> The well-known experiment, however, of the 'post-hypnotic suggestion' teaches us to insist upon the importance of the distinction between conscious and unconscious . . . a person is put into a hypnotic state and is subsequently aroused. While he was in the hypnotic state, under the influence of the physician, he was ordered to execute a certain action at a certain fixed moment after his awakening, say half an hour later. He awakes, and seems fully conscious and in his ordinary condition, he

has no recollection of his hypnotic state, and yet at the pre-arranged moment there rushes into his mind the impulse to do such and such a thing, and he does it consciously, though not knowing why.

(Freud 1958: 261)

Thus the phenomenon of post-hypnotic suggestion implies that we can be motivated by something of which we are unaware. Moreover, the observation that people under hypnosis remember previously forgotten events, strengthens the proposition that not all mental life is accessible to conscious awareness. If one accepts the legitimacy of the unconscious then much of Freud's corroborating evidence and theoretical elaboration falls into place quite neatly.

The question of the relationship between the conscious and unconscious was crucial for Freud, and once again we find him looking to hypnosis for the initial clues:

When, in 1889, I took part in the extraordinarily impressive demonstrations by Liebeault and Bernheim at Nancy, I witnessed the following experience among others. If a man was put into a state of somnambulism, was made to experience all kinds of things in a hallucinatory manner, and was then woken up, he appeared at first to know nothing of what had happened during his hypnotic sleep. . . . But Bernheim brought urgent pressure to bear on him, insisted that he knew it and must remember it. And, lo and behold! the man grew uncertain, began to reflect, and recalled in a shadowy way one of the experiences that had been suggested to him, and then another piece, and the memory became clearer and clearer and more complete.

(Freud 1973a: 132)

In such efforts to promote the recall of hypnotic experiences, the permeability of unconscious memory was demonstrated. This was important for Freud because it meant that, at least in principle, the unconscious was accessible to the conscious person. It remained for Freud to identify the importance of the unconscious in psychic life, how it operates and how to gain access to it. His own assessment of his contribution is testimony to the centrality of the unconscious 'What I discovered was the scientific method by which the unconscious can be studied' (quoted in Jahoda 1977: 16).

Initially Freud used hypnosis to bring to the surface the hidden, or forgotten, or unrecognised, thoughts and feelings of his patients. Breuer's earlier work with Anna O had demonstrated the benefits of hypnosis, especially when she was able to express the strong emotions which these forgotten thoughts had induced in her. But Freud finally abandoned hypnosis because of his conviction that at the heart of the therapeutic process was the relationship between the patient and the therapist. The core of this relationship is the phenomenon of 'transference' whereby the patient transfers on to the therapist the intense feelings previously associated with parents and other authority figures:

> We mean a transference of feelings on to the person of the doctor, since we do not believe that the situation in the treatment could justify the development of such feelings. We suspect, on the contrary, that the whole readiness for these feelings is derived from elsewhere, that they were already prepared in the patient and, upon the opportunity offered by the analytic treatment, are transferred on to the person of the doctor.
>
> (Freud 1973a: 494)

Psychoanalysis hinges around the phenomenon of transference. Patients are encouraged to work through their transference feelings and the therapist identifies the real-life triggers of these feelings. Thus it is crucial for the therapist to remain neutral with no social contact, otherwise real and neurotic feelings towards the therapist will be mixed.

The feelings expressed by the patient towards the therapist, together with the associations they trigger in the patient's mind, are the clues to unravelling the meaning of the patient's symptoms. In this way the analyst can identify repressed material and bring it to consciousness. In a passage from the case study of Dora, Freud remarks:

> He that has eyes to see and ears to hear may convince himself that no mortal can keep a secret. If his lips are silent, he chatters with his fingertips; betrayal oozes out of him at every pore. And thus the task of making conscious the most hidden recesses of the mind is one which is quite possible to accomplish.
>
> (Freud 1953: 77–8)

Psychoanalysis is thus an interpretative art based upon establishing connections between the recall, associations, feelings and symptoms of the patient. A fundamental principle is that nothing in mental life occurs randomly and that meaning can be found in the apparently trivial (such as a slip of the tongue), the bizarre (such as a compulsion to wash one's hands fifty times a day) and the commonplace (recalling number 46 as 64). Patients are thus encouraged to report whatever comes to their mind, no matter how trivial or embarrassing.

Freud discovered that when patients gave free expression to each and every thought that occurred to them, they often recounted traumatic sexual experiences which occurred during childhood. There was a time when he thought that neurosis in adults could be traced to childhood sexual encounters. We then found that the reluctance of his patients to describe these incidents, and the vague and unsatisfactory manner in which they did so, indicated that they were fabricated. They were not actual events, rather, they were the fantasies and wishes of his patients. Freud reasoned that these fantasies and wishes were caused by forces of a kind capable of accounting for their sexual tinge. This force, or energy, he called libido, which is a broadly conceived sexual energy. One should remember that by 'sexuality' Freud meant a kind of kinaesthetic pleasure to be derived from bodily stimulation. From this notion followed the idea that sexual energy is directed at different bodily zones in the course of psychological development, which led to the well-known psychosexual stages: the oral, anal, phallic and genital, and the celebrated Oedipus complex. The significance of these stages is twofold. First, there is a difference between the way males and females negotiate the course of psychosexual development, a difference which accounts for male and female adult identity. Second, there is the more general argument that if the libido is blocked or frustrated at any stage, the outcome will be an indelible mark on adult personality. For example, if an infant is deprived of oral satisfaction (sucking), a portion of the libido will become fixated at this stage and subsequently expressed in adult behaviour (e.g. excessive eating or smoking). Thus many facets of adult behaviour can be understood in terms of infantile wishes and frustrations.

If we accept Freud's view that earlier childhood experiences are often evoked by situations which resemble the past, then it is easy to see how the adult teaching–learning situation can become fraught with emotional turmoil. Many of the anxieties expressed by adult learners can be construed as having their roots in childhood and infancy. This can be illustrated by considering some of the common expectations held about teachers. Salzberger-Wittenberg *et al.* (1983) outline five such expectations:

1 The teacher as the source of knowledge and wisdom.
2 The teacher as a provider and comforter.
3 The teacher as an object of admiration and envy.
4 The teacher as a judge.
5 The teacher as an authority figure.

The argument is that each of these expectations are associated with childhood feelings, especially towards the parents. In their extreme form they represent hopes or fantasies which can never be fulfilled. The anxiety associated with them, and the inevitable disappointment, will find expression in some way – usually as a transference of hostility and other feelings towards the teacher. The following passage refers to the expectation that a teacher is both 'provider' and 'comforter':

Teachers like others in helping professions, such as e.g. doctors, nurses, psychiatrists and social workers, easily become objects of infantile hopes: someone who will magically cure pain, take away frustration, helplessness, despair, and instead provide happiness and the fulfilment of all desires. We must expect that a person who holds on to the belief that such wishes should and can be met will easily feel disappointed, may soon turn away from us in anger, blame us for being totally unhelpful and seek out someone who appears more likely to comply with his wishes. What is so dangerous in this attitude, and our tendency to fit in with it, is that it is anti-development, for as long as there is a persistent belief that the individual does not have to struggle with some frustration and mental pain he is not likely to discover or develop any latent strengths.

(Salzberger-Wittenberg *et al.* 1983: 28)

The teacher too will bring to the classroom a set of expectations, fears and aspirations, and it is important to distinguish between those that are based on unworked-over childhood conflicts and those based on positive learning and childhood experiences. Among other things, teachers fear criticism, hostility and losing control – all these are realistic fears and there is an ever-present danger that the teacher's response will be infantile (e.g. refusing to admit an error, becoming overly apologetic and self-effacing about a small mishandling of an event, not being able to criticise students' work, attacking students). Once again, Salzberger-Wittenberg *et al.* supply a nice illustration:

[Teaching] may stimulate the infantile aspects of our own personality. If the teacher has not sufficiently worked through these, he [*sic*] may become identified with the pupil's demand that all his desires should be fulfilled and endlessly gratified. The teacher may, for instance, agree that students need 'spoon-feeding' and thus be inclined to do most of the work for them. He may not realise that, in acceding to their infantile wishes, he is not only pampering them and undermining their innate capacities, but at the same time satisfying his own wish that learning should be easy. Equally, a teacher who has been, or longed to be, his parents' special child may gain vicarious satisfaction when he bestows special attention on his favourite pupil. (The rest of the class will have to suffer the pangs of jealousy which the teacher has never been able to cope with adequately.) These modes of behaviour encourage dependency and hamper students from coming to grips with reality. . . .

The inclination to indulge students may receive further reinforcement from the teacher's fear that any frustration will lead to an outburst of unlimited anger. If the teacher himself is inclined to react with violent rage to the absence of gratification, it will make him so frightened of his students' hostile attacks that he may be unable to enforce limits.

(Salzberger-Wittenberg *et al.* 1983: 50)

I have been able to provide some empirical support for the above position through documenting the annoyances, guilt feelings and fears expressed by adult educators working in a range of different contexts (Tennant 1991a,

1991b). The common guilt feelings of the teachers were the failure to meet needs, lack of preparation, and the inability to manage relationships of authority and control. Common fears were the inability to meet needs, inadequate expertise or knowledge, and poor teaching and organisational skills. Common annoyances were the failure of learners to participate, learners violating the 'terms' of participation, and learners rejecting the content or the process.

In a different analysis Williams (1993) locates classroom dynamics in the tensions present in the patriarchal family:

> I use the analogy of the patriarchal family to illustrate the sorts of dynamics that can be generated from a culturally constructed set of gendered power relations and role expectations. Continuing the analogy, the question of the part the institution plays in this dynamic arises. In the family triad 'dad' is, of course, the ultimate authority, the institution itself. Feminist and humanist teachers often experience split loyalties as does 'mum' in trying to attend to the needs of both the child/student and father/institution. . . . When teachers side with the institution/father against the student/child, in order to protect their own interests, the student/child cannot help but feel betrayed. In such circumstances the student's anger and hostility toward the teacher is quite understandable.
>
> (Williams 1993: 57–8)

Williams also points to the contradictory nature of teaching: to provide a 'safe' and 'comfortable' environment for learners while at the same time extending and challenging their beliefs, assumptions and knowledge. The challenge for adult educators is to disperse authority, control and decision making among learners without losing a sense of their own identity as a teacher

Basic psychoanalytic concepts, then, can be applied to understanding the dynamics of the classroom. In particular, notions such as the unconscious, the predominance of childhood psychic life and transference, can be used to make sense of the 'emotionality' of teaching and learning and the ways in which this finds expression.

INDIVIDUAL IDENTITY AND SOCIETY

Freud's view of the relationship between person and society needs to be understood in the context of his description of the basic structures of personality. Briefly, he distinguishes between three components of personality: the id, ego and super-ego. Only the id is present at birth. It is a reservoir of instinctual energy. It has no direction; it is illogical, unorganised; it is simply a mass of excitation. It operates according to the primary process, which discharges instinctual energy without regard to reality. Its goal is twofold, to reduce the excitation of the organism (the Nirvana principle) and to increase affective pleasure and decrease affective unpleasure or pain (the pleasure principle). In attaining these goals, all it can do is wish. This may result in short-term tension reduction, but ultimately the organism must take reality into account if its wishes are to be fulfilled.

The development of the ego arises from this need to perceive reality. The ego also pursues pleasure and seeks to avoid unpleasure or pain. However, it operates according to the reality principle: it perceives, remembers, thinks and acts on the world. It performs a mediating role between the demands of the instinct and the action that will satisfy it. The ego adapts to reality, and part of this reality is social. Thus the ego must *understand* the moral and ethical codes of society, its values, ideals and taboos. Such an understanding is necessary for the ego to appraise the consequences of a given course of action. For example, violating a moral code in the pursuit of pleasure will result in some form of punishment by an external agent, usually the parent. A crucial point for Freud is that in the course of development, sanctions for wrong-doing come to be administered internally via one's conscience. Thus emerges the third component of personality structure, the super-ego.

> Even if conscience is something 'within us' yet it is not so from the first. In this it is a real contrast to sexual life, which is in fact there from the beginning of life and not only a later addition. But, as is well known, young children are amoral and possess no internal inhibitions against their impulses striving for pleasure. The part which is later taken on by the super-ego is played to begin with by an external power, by parental authority. . . . It is only subsequently that the secondary situation develops where the external restraint is internalized and the super-ego takes the place of the parental agency and observes, directs and threatens the ego in exactly the same way as earlier the parents did with the child.
>
> (Freud 1973b: 93)

The super-ego represents the claims of morality; it is the internal means of judging good from bad. Thoughts or actions which violate social prescriptions are censured by the conscience and feelings of guilt or shame are generated. In contrast, thoughts or actions which approximate the ego ideal (an idealised abstraction of parental or social values) give rise to feelings of pride and self-esteem.

The above view of personality structure implies that there is a necessary conflict between person and society. This is because the basic instincts, which derive from bodily needs, are essentially anti-social. The person is caught in a dilemma. Other people are necessary for instinctual gratification but the co-operation of others is not possible without ordered social life. Yet ordered social life presupposes a degree of instinctual renunciation (for example, the restriction of aggressiveness). A unique insight of Freud was his claim that the external conflict between person and society becomes transformed into an internal psychological conflict between the structures within the personality. This is expressed in the following passage from *Civilization and its Discontents*:

> Another question concerns us more nearly. What means does civilization employ in order to inhibit the aggressiveness which opposes it, to make it harmless, to get rid of it, perhaps? We have already become acquainted with a few of these methods, but not yet with the one that appears to be the most important. This we can study in the history of the development of the individual. What happens in him to render his desire for aggression innocuous? Something very remarkable, which we should never have guessed and which is nevertheless quite obvious. His aggressiveness is interjected, internalized; it is, in point of fact, sent back to where it came from – that is, it is directed towards his own ego. There it is taken over by a portion of the ego, which sets itself over against the rest of the ego as super-ego, and which now, in the form of 'conscience', is ready to put into action against the ego the same harsh aggressiveness that the ego would have liked to satisfy upon other, extraneous individuals. The tension between the harsh super-ego and the ego that is subjected to it, is called by us the sense of guilt; it expresses itself as a need for punishment. Civilization, therefore, obtains mastery over the individual's dangerous desire for aggression by weakening and disarming it and by setting up an agency within him to watch over it, like a garrison in a conquered city.
>
> (Freud 1963: 60–1)

This explains a later remark by Freud that the price we pay for civilisation is a heightened sense of guilt. And it also places in perspective Fromm's comment on the truly tragic picture of history that Freud presents.

> Progress, beyond a certain point ... is in principle impossible. Man is only a battlefield on which the life and death instincts fight each other. He can never liberate himself decisively from the tragic alternative of destroying others or himself.
>
> (Fromm 1973: 66)

Freud, it seems, set an upper limit on our capacity for happiness and psychological health. This social thrust within psychoanalysis was both developed and challenged by subsequent work within the psychoanalytic tradition. The politically radical psychoanalytic thinkers such as Reich (1972) and Marcuse (1969) reject the idea that instinctual gratification and ordered social life are incompatible. They regard repression (and its associated concepts such as the Oedipus complex), not as a necessary product of the human condition, but as the product of a specific type of social organisation, namely, the patriarchal authoritarian one. For example, Reich claims that anti-social impulses such as aggression are secondary, resulting from the repression of natural biological needs. He thus rejects the notion of anti-social instincts.

> Moral regulation represses and keeps from gratification the natural biological needs. This results in secondary pathological anti-social impulses. These in turn have to be inhibited of necessity. Thus, morality does not owe its existence to the necessity of inhibiting anti-social tendencies.
>
> (Reich 1972: 22)

In *Eros and Civilisation*, Marcuse (1969) points out that Freud failed to distinguish between the level of repression required to maintain society as such, and the level required to support an oppressive social structure. Both Reich and Marcuse tapped the critical force of psychoanalysis and recognised its potential as a basis for a theory of oppression – as did others much later (e.g. the women's movement and Marxist intellectuals). Connell (1983) explores this theme in his essay 'Dr Freud and the course of history', where he draws an analogy between the psychoanalytic technique of 'decoding' the meanings of unconscious material produced by patients (e.g. dreams and symptoms) and the Marxist analysis of ideology. In the latter, many common-sense, everyday understandings of life are 'decoded' or 'unmasked' as distortions which serve to conceal domination and exploitation.

Thus the idea that we internalise the social values of our parents and other authority figures gives us a glimpse of the way in which the social structure is united to constraints that operate in our personality. It assists us in explaining how we can act against our own best interests and how political, racial, class and sexual oppression can become a constituent part of personality structure and the conflicts within it. Connell offers the following assessment:

> It is a psychology of impossible situations, where irresistible forces of lust and rage meet immovable obstacles of social relations and culture, and produce our lives as a result. It is a theory, in fact the only theory, that begins to account for the way oppressive situations are lived by the people in them, the way consciousness itself is distorted by psychological force majeure.
>
> (Connell 1983: 15)

Freud's characterisation of the relationship between person and society is crucially important. The link between social oppression and psychological repression has occupied the attention of adult educators working with oppressed groups (e.g. Freire 1972; Thompson 1983). Psychoanalysis offers us a theory which explains why some members of oppressed groups fail to recognise their oppression and may angrily denounce those who attempt to convince them otherwise (organisations like 'Women Who Want to be Women' provide a collective outlet for such a denunciation). A key issue for adult educators working with oppressed groups is how best to conceive their role. One approach is to consider adult education as a kind of therapeutic exercise which offers relief from the symptoms of repression/oppression by, say, 'assisting with personal growth' or 'building confidence'. Keddie has criticised the conservatism of this approach:

> Confidence for what or in what? Is adult education, through providing a 'woman's interest' curriculum, enabling women to become more satisfied consumers of their own oppression? Is it making them more confident and competent managers of their homes, more able to cope with its tensions through courses in Yoga, slimmer and more attractive through Keep Fit and Beauty Culture, and meeting their needs for self-expression through classes in painting or creative writing? Does providing women with an interest outside the home and a crèche for classes, give them a break from the children which makes them happier mothers and create more lively and informed wives who can show more interest in their husbands' work?
>
> (Keddie, cited in Thompson 1983: 84)

The alternative is for the adult educator to become actively engaged in social change. Initially this may be done by creating among learners a critical awareness of the oppressive nature of their position. A commitment to this approach brings with it the issue of how the adult educator can best assist in this process – an issue which will be addressed in Chapter 9. All this seems rather remote from psychoanalysis, but it is worth emphasising that psychological repression can be interpreted as a response to forms of social oppression.

ERIKSON'S 'PSYCHOSOCIAL' STAGES: A PSYCHOANALYTIC APPROACH TO ADULT DEVELOPMENT

Erikson (1959) describes personality growth in terms of a sequence of stages which he labels 'psychosocial stages'. As development proceeds, the ego alters to meet the changing demands of society. This need to adjust to society's demands promotes an emotional crisis or conflict within the person. Erikson identifies eight basic crises across the life span, each one corresponding to a stage of development as outlined in Table 3.1.

Erikson's earlier stages complement the psychosexual stages of Freud. For example, he regards the oral–sensory stage as being one where the child 'lives through and lives with, his mouth. . . . To him the mouth is the

Table 3.1 Erikson's stages of psychosocial development

Psychosocial stage	Characteristic emotional crisis
Oral–sensory	Basic trust vs mistrust
Anal–musculature	Autonomy vs shame, doubt
Genital–locomotor	Initiative vs guilt
Latency	Industry vs inferiority
Puberty and adolescence	Identity vs role confusion
Young adulthood	Intimacy vs isolation
Adulthood	Generativity vs stagnation
Maturity	Ego integrity vs despair

Source: adapted from Erikson (1959)

focus of a general first approach to life – the incorporative approach' (Erikson 1959: 57). At this stage, the child's ego must be capable of dealing with the wealth of sensory experiences that it encounters. If these experiences are basically pleasant, the child will feel the world is benign and supportive: the child will develop a sense of basic trust. If the sensory experiences result in pain and discomfort and the world appears to be a place of pain and danger – then a sense of mistrust will develop. The remaining childhood stages of development also have close parallels with Freud's psychosexual stages. During the anal–musculature stage the principal crisis centres on the child's capacity to control its bodily movement and thereby develop a sense of autonomy. Shame and doubt will result from lack of control (e.g. of bowel movements), shame because of others' disapproval, and doubt because of one's feeling of incompetence. The genital stage has close links with Freud's phallic stage: the child, in resolving its Oedipal conflict (i.e. the conflict between rivalry and identification with the same sex), is drawn into a general crisis of initiative (which is an expression of independence from parental ties) versus guilt (where a continued dependence on parents is in conflict with society's expectations). The latency stage is a time when children are expected to acquire the basic skills which prepare them for adult life; in western society this takes the form of schooling. The sense of industry or inferiority is predicated on the child's capacity to acquire these skills. Finally, the stage of puberty and adolescence corresponds to the genital stage in Freudian theory. Unlike Freud, who is primarily concerned with the emergence of a genital sex drive, Erikson is concerned with the implications of all the changes which occur during adolescence (i.e. physiological and physical changes together with the changing expectations of society). These changes result in an identity crisis for adolescents. They are confronted with the task of defining themselves and making a commitment to their social roles; failure to do so results in identity confusion. At this point, the parallels with Freudian psychosexual stages cease and Erikson describes a further three stages of adult development. The first adult stage, young adulthood, centres on the crisis of intimacy. Will the developing person have the capacity to form intimate relationships with others or will he or she become self-absorbed? The answer depends largely on the outcome of earlier crises, in particular, the identity crisis of adolescence.

> But it is only after a reasonable sense of identity has been established that real intimacy with the other sex (or, for that matter, with any other person or even with oneself) is possible. . . the condition of a true twoness is that one must first become oneself.
>
> (Erikson 1959: 95)

The next stage, adulthood, focuses on whether the person has a sense of being a productive, contributing member of society (generativity) or whether the person feels unable to contribute (stagnation). In the final stage, integrity is the culmination of the successful resolution of life's developmental crises. 'It is the acceptance of one's own and only life cycle . . . it is a sense of comradeship with men and women of distant times and of different pursuits' (Erikson 1959: 98). Opposed to integrity is the sense of despair which is characterised by a fear of death and a failure to accept one's personal history.

Even though Erikson emphasises changing social demands as being the catalyst for individual growth and development, he does not dispense with the (psychoanalytic) view that maturation plays a central role. He maintains that the human organism has a 'ground plan' which obeys 'inner laws of development'.

> Personality can be said to develop according to steps predetermined in the human organism's readiness to be driven forward, to be aware of, and to interact with a widening social radius.
>
> (Erikson 1959: 52)

Thus personality development is governed by a maturational timetable. This means that the development of capabilities like trust, autonomy, initiative and industry, occur only during critical periods of life. If these capabilities do not emerge when they are supposed to, then their optimum development will be impaired and subsequent development will be unfavourably affected. That is, intimacy is predicated on identity, identity upon industry and industry upon initiative, etc.

To sum up, the psychosocial stages occur in an invariant sequence, and the resolution of each successive crisis leaves an indelible impression on personality, which moreover influences the resolution of subsequent crises.

The outcome of the successful resolution of life's developmental crises is the healthy integrated personality. The healthy personality charts a course through each crisis 'emerging and re-emerging with an increased sense of inner unity, with an increase of good judgement and an increase in the capacity to do well, according to the standards of those who are significant to him' (Erikson 1959: 51).

Erikson's theory broadens and extends the Freudian psychosexual stages through a focus on the emergence of identity and a stress on the impact of social demands. Similarly, his concept of the healthy personality is cast more positively than Freud's, instead of being a compromise between instinctual gratification and the demands of social life, the healthy personality emerges from the positive resolution of a series of emotional crises. Nevertheless, Erikson's theory is firmly entrenched in the psychoanalytic tradition; testimony to this is the use of psychoanalytic concepts and the importance attached to maturation and the experience of childhood. Like Freud, he postulates a structure of ego development which is universal: it is only the psychological *content* of the crisis resolutions which are cultural and historical. In this sense, his theory is as rigid as Freud's.

The most important critique of Erikson (Jacoby 1975; Roazen 1976) is that his theory is conformist and supports the status quo. Even though he expresses an awareness of alienating and repressive social forces, his view of psychological health is couched in terms of how well the person adapts to society's needs. Thus Buss remarks:

> I can imagine a society where the more valid reaction is shame and doubt rather than autonomy, guilt rather than initiative, identity diffusion rather than identity. The conflict and confusions that an individual experiences may represent a healthy response to a social reality that is psychologically (not to mention physically) repressive, alienating and constricting. Integration of the individual into society is not an absolute to be unquestioningly sought after.
>
> (Buss 1979: 328)

Ironically, while Erikson seeks to avoid the ahistorical nature of orthodox psychoanalysis, the alternative he offers is an ahistorical view of the healthy personality as one which adapts to the demands of a particular social/historical world. In rejecting Freud's pessimistic view, which allows little scope for progress in the human condition, Erikson portrays the person–society relationship as one characterised by harmony – and the development of a healthy personality is predicated on this harmony.

Both Erikson and Freud have much to say about the relationship between individual psychology and social organisation, but neither develops a social critique. Freud considers internal psychological conflict to be a necessary product of civilisation – *any* civilisation – thus mental health and happiness is limited by civilisation *per se*. Erikson sees mental health as attainable but defines it in terms of how people successfully adjust to the demands of society. The possibility that some forms of social organisation are alienating and psychologically unhealthy, while others are liberating and psychologically healthy, was not systematically explored by them. This theme was elaborated by later more radical psychoanalytic thinkers who latched on to the social thrust of psychoanalysis – a thrust which is still being developed and which is apparent, at least implicitly, in the thinking of some adult educators.

Chapter 4

The development of identity during adulthood

Adult educators, who in many respects are critical consumers of ideas about teaching and learning, seem to have a weakness when it comes to critically evaluating theory and research in adult development. This weakness is perhaps due to the belief that the identity of adult education is premised on the identity of the adult. Hence the literature on adult development is attractive because it offers (however illusory the offer may be) the promise of a distinct and coherent theory of adult learning.

Published accounts of the adult learning process nearly always make reference to life span developmental stages, the life cycle or the 'phases' of adult life. In a similar way many policy documents in adult and continuing education stress the importance of addressing the needs associated with adult development and growth. This is because much of adult education is either explicitly or implicitly concerned with adult development. A range of programmes directly address life-span issues arising from gender roles, marriage, parenting, health, retirement, sexuality, migration, elderly people, unemployment and so on. Irrespective of the political and social origins of the discrimination and exploitation associated with these areas, educators at some stage have to attend to their psychological impact and have a view about the possibility of transformation at the individual psychological level. Allman (1982) sets out the case for this interest in adult development. She observes that studies of adult life reveal it to be a period of change and development, much like that of childhood and adolescence. She argues that the results of such studies serve notice on the prevailing assumptions about adulthood – that it is a long period of stability where previously learned capacities, skills, attitudes and values are applied to one's activities at work, in the family, in leisure and in civic life. These assumptions need to be challenged because they 'clearly affect decision makers in the field of politics, education and social policy' (Allman 1982: 42). In education they are linked to the conventional view that the period of initial education equips young adults for the remainder of their working lives – a view which continues to inform political debate on educational priorities. There is also a need, according to Allman, to disseminate knowledge about adult development to the community at large:

> It is also urgent that these ideas begin to permeate the realm of common sense, as all adults are continually in the process of making personal life decisions which may be based on similar highly questionable assumptions about their own potential for growth and development.
>
> (Allman 1982: 43)

Arguments like these are convincing and we do need to revise our outmoded views about adult life. But, as I shall argue, we need to proceed with caution, otherwise there is a risk of replacing one set of false beliefs with another equally false (albeit more palatable) set of beliefs about adult development.

The first part of this chapter reviews some of the connections which have been made between adult development and adult education. The second part focuses on evaluating the adequacy of existing theory and research in this area.

A question commonly posed by those with an interest in adult learning is: 'What are the implications of adult development for adult and continuing education practitioners?' Knox (1979) outlines three possible implications:

1 To predict and explain success in education: 'Practitioners are typically interested in developmental generalizations regarding performance or personality in order to predict and explain successful participation in educative activity' (Knox 1979: 59).
2 To help people adapt to changing adult roles: 'Adult life cycle trends in performance in family, occupational and community roles suggest ways in which continuing education participation might facilitate adaptation and growth related to each role area' (Knox 1979: 59).
3 To improve the effectiveness of marketing and instructional activities: 'From time to time, the stability of adulthood is punctuated by role change events such as the birth of the first child, a move to another community or retirement. . . . Such change events typically produce heightened readiness to learn which, if recognized, can contribute to the effectiveness of marketing and instructional activities' (Knox 1979: 60).

The whole tenor of the above implications indicates a view about adult development and an attitude to adult education. That is, that the various 'roles' of adult life are inevitable and people must learn to cope with them as they arise; and that adult education agencies, if they wish to be successful, should gear their marketing and instructional activities to cater for the different needs of adults at different life stages. There is no sense in which adult roles are portrayed as arbitrary or even oppressive, or that alternative roles and options are possible for a given life period. In this sense adult education contributes towards the maintenance of social norms and structures. One need not look very far to find other instances of this type of approach. A significant example can be found in McCoy's (1977) tabulation of *Adult Life Cycle Tasks and Educational Program Responses* which is reproduced in Chickering's (1981) influential volume *The Modern American College*. McCoy identifies seven developmental stages, each of which is characterised by a set of common tasks. For example, the 'leaving home' stage (18–22) has the associated tasks of 'break psychological ties', 'choose career', 'enter work', 'manage time' and so on. Each stage is then related to an appropriate range of programme responses, with a final column indicating the outcomes sought from the educational programme. The table is too lengthy to reproduce here, but a cross-section of one stage only will be sufficient to illustrate the general strategy. Table 4.1 shows the 'tasks' and 'programme responses' appropriate for the developmental stage 'Becoming adult'.

A casual glance at the list of tasks and how each of them relates to specified programmes confirms my general point about adult education supporting the status quo. Even a non-specific 'task' such as 'achieving autonomy' is interpreted in the most narrow sense possible, that is, as the capacity to 'live alone successfully'. It is unnecessary to elaborate further; the tabulation speaks for itself. What is surprising, and disappointing, is that anyone in adult education would take such an analysis seriously as anything other than a narrow descriptive exercise.

Yet there is a strongly held view among adult educators that the everyday reality of learners should be acknowledged, no matter how culturally specific that reality may be. The reader may remonstrate that McCoy is simply following this precept – what, then, is so objectionable? As I see it, there are two objections. The first of these is that there is no acknowledgement of the narrow culturally specific 'tasks' which are identified. Quite the opposite, the 'tasks' are presented as a generalisable framework to be used by adult education agencies in formulating their programmes. There is no sense in which McCoy is using her analysis as a case study of a process for others to emulate in a different cultural context. The second objection, already mentioned in relation to Knox, is that the response of adult education is depicted as solely adaptive. There is no scope for questioning and challenging the tasks – they constitute the taken for granted reality of the learners *and* the adult educators.

There are many adult educators who, being dismissive of the above approach, nevertheless subscribe to the view that adult development is a central concept in adult education. An interest in adult development stems quite naturally from a commitment to the notion of lifelong learning and the associated concepts of 'lifelong education', 'recurrent education' and 'education permanent'. The policy and research documents of UNESCO, the OECD and the Council of Europe, which are the major sponsoring

Table 4.1 Educational responses to life cycle tasks

	Tasks	Programme response
1	Select mate	Marriage workshops
2	Settle in work, begin career ladder	Management, advancement training
3	Parent	Parenting workshops
4	Become involved in community	Civic education, volunteer training
5	Consume wisely	Consumer education, financial management training
6	Home-own	Home-owning, maintenance workshops
7	Socially interact	Human relations groups, TA (transactional analysis)
8	Achieve autonomy	Living alone, divorce workshops
9	Problem solve	Creative problem-solving workshops
10	Manage stress accompanying change	Stress management, biofeedback, relaxation, TM (transcendental meditation) workshops

Source: McCoy (1977)

bodies of these concepts, frequently cite adult development as a central concern of any lifelong learning strategy. However, they do not understand adult development to be an immutable sequence of stages through which people pass at more or less predictable ages. Indeed, they challenge the concept of the 'typical' life cycle and support their view with an analysis of contemporary social and economic change. This is particularly apparent in the literature on recurrent education, and the following extract, taken from an article by one of its chief proponents, Jarl Bengtsson, typifies this approach:

> significant changes are taking place in the relationship between work and non-work time seen over the individual's whole life cycle in terms of increased education, earlier retirement, longer holidays, etc. It has also been made clear that these changes affect social groups according to their hierarchical position in working life, as well as the way their work is being scheduled, i.e. full-time, part-time, shift work, long spells of employment, etc.
>
> The claim is not that more non-work time is or will be used for education, although that certainly remains a strong possibility. Rather it is that to look at recurrent education from this perspective provides a very useful point of departure for placing it in the broader context of emerging new life-styles and life cycles. Most likely, the crucial factors behind changes in the individual's life cycle pattern will be the economic and employment conditions that the industrialized countries will face during coming years.
>
> (Bengtsson 1979: 26)

Recurrent education, and its closely related concepts, accepts the diversity

of life cycle patterns and the need for educational institutions to respond
to and foster this diversity through a diversity of provision. It supports
the notion that individual options should be extended, especially the way
in which paid work, unpaid work, education and leisure are combined.
The principles espoused can be seen as a response to the effects of social,
economic and technological change. Changes in demographic patterns,
the sexual division of labour, the length of working life, hours spent at
work, retirement age and so on, are all seen as relevant to the proposition
that educational opportunities should be distributed, in a recurring way,
across the life span. Recurrent education also embodies the notion of social
justice and its evolution as a concept from the late 1960s has been linked
with a host of terms implying broad social reforms: industrial democracy,
participation in planning, social equity, decentralisation, links between
education and work and between younger and older generations, and
concern with the disadvantaged. An underlying value in all this is a
humanistic concern for the individual. The idea of self-development,
which is based on notions of individuality and growth, is contrasted with
the opposing notions of enslavement, alienation and stagnation – which
are the psychological consequences of clinging to an outmoded conception
of the 'normal' life cycle.

Research and theory in adult development is not always concerned with
identifying so called 'normal' life patterns. A bevy of theoretical perspectives and research techniques have been deployed to make sense of the
experience of adulthood. The resulting literature is diverse and difficult to
harness, especially for adult educators who often want only to apply a few
general (and unambiguous) principles to their practice. Generally speaking, however, the narrowly focused, neatly presented and least ambiguous
'principles' are those which are the most questionable. This theme will now
be expanded and illustrated more thoroughly in the remainder of this
chapter.

There are two persistent problems which are a feature of adult developmental psychology. The first is that there are insurmountable methodological difficulties in establishing 'phases' or 'stages' of adult life. The
second is that much of the literature is historically and socially rooted and
lacks any worthwhile generalisability.

METHODOLOGICAL DIFFICULTIES

I have dealt elsewhere in the text with some of the conceptual and
methodological problems in stage-development research. Not all adult
development studies adopt a stage-sequence approach; nevertheless, they
usually have a stake in making comparisons between different 'ages',
'phases' or 'stages' of life. Leaving aside the problem of deciding what
types of data to gather, the common methodological problem is to

construct a research design which generates comparative data (on whatever dimension) which indicate the effects of age changes only (where the effects of other factors, such as 'history' and 'time of measurement', are neutralised). Many of the most influential studies in adult development use research designs which fail to do this. Three basic research designs are the 'cross-sectional', 'longitudinal' and 'time-lag' designs. These are illustrated in Figure 4.1.

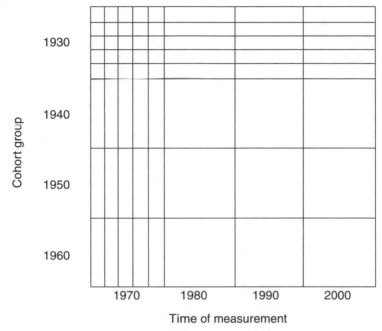

Figure 4.1 Adult development: basic research designs

The cross-sectional design is represented by each of the columns. It is where two or more age cohorts are investigated at *one* time of measurement. The hypothetical example in the figure appears in the left hand column, where at one time of measurement (1970) data are gathered from four age cohorts (people born in 1930, 1940, 1950, 1960). Perhaps the best known example of this technique is to be found in the research of Gould (1972). In an initial study Gould (1972) observed and recorded the concerns expressed by a number of psychiatric outpatients. He hypothesised that these concerns differed among different age groups. He then used these expressed concerns to construct a questionnaire which contained 160 questions divided into ten areas of life. This questionnaire was then administered, in a later study, to a sample of 524 non-patients, who were white middle-class men and women aged 16–50 years. They were required to rank a selection of statements according to their personal applicability, as shown in Table 4.2.

The difficulty with a research design such as this is that the observed differences in 'concerns' may be due to the different life experiences of the different age cohorts. For example, the life history of a 50-year-old person in 1972 would necessarily include the 'great depression' of the 1930s and the experience of the Second World War. This would be quite different from the life history of a 22-year-old person in 1972 who would have experienced (as a child and youth) the economic boom of the post-war years and the social changes of the 1960s. It seems reasonable to assume that such historical events and trends affect people's 'concerns'. Indeed they may be more significant in explaining the different concerns of different age cohorts than any hypothesised notion of the life cycle.

One way to avoid making comparisons between different cohorts is to investigate a single age cohort over a number of years. This is referred to as a longitudinal design and is represented by the rows in Figure 4.1. The horizontal lines on the top row provide a hypothetical example. A sample of people born in 1930 could be studied at different times, in 1970 (40 years), 1980 (50 years), 1990 (60 years) and 2000 (70 years). The Grant Study (Vaillant 1977; Vaillant and Vaillant 1990) provides a good example of this type of research design. A group of 173 graduates from the early 1940s were followed through from the age of 18 years to 65 years. They were part of an initial study of 268 male undergraduates who were given extensive physiological and psychological examinations early in their college years. After graduation a sample of graduates completed annual

Table 4.2 A sample of statements from Gould's questionnaire

1	I feel that some exciting things are going to happen to me.
2	I never plan on what tomorrow may bring.
3	It hurts me to realise that I will not get some things in life I want.
4	I live for today, forget the past.
5	I think things aren't as good as they used to be.
6	I believe I will some day have everything I want in life.
7	My life doesn't change much from year to year.
8	There is little hope for the future.
9	I try to be satisfied about what I have and not to think so much about the things I probably won't be able to get.
10	I wish I could change the past.
11	I dream about life ten years from now.
12	I spend more time now thinking about the past than about the future.
13	There's still plenty of time to do most of the things I want to do.
14	I would be quite content to remain as old as I am now.
15	I find myself daydreaming about good experiences in the past.
16	I will have to settle for less than I expected, but I still think I will get most things I want.

Source: Gould (1972: 527)

questionnaires until 1955, and every two years after that date. They were also interviewed at ages 25, 30, 47, 57 and 65. Vaillant (1977; see also Vaillant and Vaillant 1990) reports the results in detail, but his thesis is simple: that ego defence mechanisms mature through the life cycle and that healthy adults progress through a hierarchy of adaptive mechanisms as shown in Table 4.3.

There are some well-documented problems with longitudinal studies, such as experimental mortality (where participants drop out of the study) and practice effects (where the participants become overly familiar with the style of the questionnaire and the structure of the interview) and time-of-measurement effects (where measurements, because they are taken at different times, may reflect only changed social and cultural conditions). A significant problem, and one often overlooked, is that over, say, a thirty-year period, there are bound to be shifts in the theoretical perspective of the theory upon which the research is based. This often means that the initial questions and modes of analysis become obsolescent and are replaced by more contemporary techniques. This certainly happened in

Table 4.3 Hierarchy of adaptive mechanisms

Level I   Psychotic mechanisms (common in psychosis, dreams, childhood)

Denial (of external reality)
Distortion
Delusional projection

Level II   Immature mechanisms (common in severe depression, personality disorders and adolescence)

Fantasy (schizoid withdrawal, denial through fantasy)
Projection
Hypochondriasis
Passive-aggressive behaviour (masochism, turning against the self)
Acting out (compulsive delinquency, perversion)

Level III   Neurotic mechanisms (common in everyone)

Intellectualisation (isolation, obsessive behaviour, undoing, relationalisation)
Repression
Reaction formation
Displacement (conversion, phobias, wit)
Dissociation (neurotic denial)

Level IV   Mature mechanisms (common in 'healthy' adults)

Sublimation
Altruism
Suppression
Anticipation
Humour

Source: Vaillant (1977: 80; see also Vaillant and Vaillant 1990)

Vaillant's study, and as he points out, had the work of Erik Erikson, Anna Freud, Harry Stack Sullivan, Melanie Klein and Heinz Hartmann been more established, it would have had a significant impact on the initial design of the Grant Study. For example it was not until the 1950s that the Grant Study began to focus on interpersonal relationships (Klein and Sullivan), and not until the 1960s did it focus on men's styles of psychological adaptation (Anna Freud and Hartmann). Also the research staff working on the project, prior to the influence of Erikson, viewed psychodynamic maturation as being completed by adolescence

Even though longitudinal studies overcome the problems of comparing different cohorts, they nevertheless remain historically bound. This means that generalisations to different cohort groups can be made only on the assumption that historical variation is unimportant.

Is it possible to avoid the influence of historical variation? The answer to this question rests heavily on one's analysis of how history and culture influence the psychological make-up of individuals. From a research design point of view it is certainly possible to control for historical effects by using some combination of longitudinal and cross-sectional designs. For example, combining the first two vertical columns in Figure 4.1 would represent a cross-sectional sequence where all four cohort groups are investigated twice, once in 1970 and again in 1980. Similarly, combining the bottom two rows would represent a longitudinal sequence, where two cohort groups are investigated simultaneously over a number of years (1970–2000). Through such techniques it is possible to obtain data about the effects of cohort differences, time-of-measurement differences and age differences. For example, the differences between 20 year olds (1970–80) can be compared with the differences between 30 year olds (1980–90) in order to gauge the effect of cohort membership on the general difference between 20 and 30 year olds. This, in effect, is a way of 'controlling' for historical variation. But the control gained through such a practice is very limited. First, it depends on whether the changes being monitored are easily quantifiable. In fact, most of the studies of this kind have been developed by those with an interest in measuring the development of human abilities, especially intellectual development (e.g. Schaie 1979). The research designs employed were initially intended to partial out the historical effects of improvements in educational provision during (longitudinal) or between (cross-sectional) the lifetimes of the subjects being studied. This is easy to do when it is simply a matter of comparing test scores, but it is a dubious task to make such comparisons with qualitative data of the kind found in adult personality development. Second, there is an assumption that the impact of history is linear and cumulative. But this is an untenable assumption (e.g. a 20 year old in 1975 may be quite different from a 20 year old in 1970 or 1980).

Another way of minimising the impact of historical variations on developmental research is to gather 'data' of a higher level of generality. Gould's questionnaire addressed those sorts of things which are historically and socially specific (views about marriage, career, children, etc.). However, other investigators have pitched their analysis at a more general level. For example, Lowenthal *et al.* (1977) used a cross-sectional technique to investigate the adaptive processes of men and women across the life span. In their study they documented such general psychological qualities as complexity, self-image, expressiveness and perceptions in continuity of value structure. The biographical interview technique of Levinson (1978) was primarily aimed at elucidating changes in the relationship between self and world throughout the life course. Loevinger (1976) was also concerned with the rather abstract notion of ego as a central frame of reference for understanding self and others. However, a closer look at this research will still reveal its social and historical specificity.

SOCIAL AND HISTORICAL BIAS

In the immediately preceding section on methodological difficulties I outlined some of the research design problems when comparing different people of different ages at a given time (cross-sectional) or when comparing the same people at different ages (longitudinal). I argued that historical events either confound the results of any comparison or they limit the generalisability of the results.

There is another, less direct way in which 'history' can affect research in adult development. Research is necessarily conducted in a particular social and historical context, but good research should produce results which are generalisable beyond that context. Unfortunately, research in adult development, especially the genre concerned with life 'stages' or 'phases', seems prone to social and historical bias. This is evident in four ways: the existence of purely descriptive inventories of life 'tasks', the selection of subjects for research, the data-gathering techniques, and the way in which the concept of the 'healthy' personality is constructed.

Descriptive inventories

Reference has already been made to McCoy's (1977) tabulation *Adult Life Cycle Tasks and Educational Program Responses*. This approach, whereby an inventory of life tasks is constructed, has its origins in Havighurst's (1972) *Developmental Tasks and Education* which was written in the early 1940s. Table 4.4 is a modified version of Havighurst's original set of developmental tasks. It is similar to the inventory of McCoy (1977) and the same objections apply here. It is worthwhile noting, however, Havighurst's comments on his original inventory.

Table 4.4 Developmental tasks of the adult years

16–23 Late adolescence and youth	23–35 Early adulthood	35–45 Midlife transition	45–57 Middle adulthood	57–65 Late adult transition	65+ Late adulthood
Achieving emotional independence					
Preparing for marriage and family life					
Choosing and preparing for a career					
Developing an ethical system					
	Deciding on a partner				
	Starting a family				
	Managing a home				
	Starting in an occupation				
	Assuming civic responsibilities				
		Adapting to a changing time perspective			
		Revising career plans			
		Redefining family relationships			
			Maintaining a career or developing a new one		
			Restabilising family relationships		
			Making mature civic contributions		
			Adjusting to biological change		
				Preparing for retirement	
					Adjusting to retirement
					Adjusting to declining health and strength
					Becoming affiliated with late-adult age groups
					Establishing satisfactory living arrangements
					Adjusting to the death of a spouse
					Maintaining integrity

Source: Chickering and Havighurst (1981: 31)

The tasks the individual must learn – the developmental tasks of life – are those things that constitute healthy and satisfactory growth in our society. They are the things a person must learn if he [sic] is to be judged and to judge himself to be a reasonably happy and successful person. A developmental task is a task which arises at or about a certain period in the life of the individual, successful achievement of which leads to his happiness and to success with later tasks, while failure leads to unhappiness in the individual, disapproval by the society, and difficulty with later tasks.

(Havighurst 1972: 2)

Thus the developmental tasks of life amount to a socially approved timetable for individual growth and development. In a pluralistic society this timetable will differ between social groups. While it may be useful to identify the developmental tasks of particular social or community groups, as Tucker and Huerta (1987) have done in their study of Mexican-American females, it is dangerous to generalise about the developmental tasks of society as such.

Sample selection, data-gathering techniques

Table 4.5 sets out the sample, method and developmental processes identified by each of seven well-known adult developmental psychologists. Five of these gathered data prior to formulating their views about adult development. An impressionistic description of the samples used is that they consisted of North American, white, middle-class, better educated, predominantly male subjects.

The techniques for gathering data were the structured interview, questionnaire, self-rating checklist, standard psychological test and observer rating. But one should be wary of accepting reported results without a detailed knowledge of how these techniques were applied in each case. For example, in reporting the results of his longitudinal study of men Vaillant (1977) at one point describes the association between psychological maturity and external adjustment. In Table 4.6 he compares the men with the 'best life outcomes' and 'worst life outcomes' (determined by an independent adjustment scale) on the dimension of psychological maturity. He compares them on the basis of how they fare on a number of 'external adjustment' indicators which include 'failure to marry by 30', 'children admitted to father's college' and 'average yearly charitable contribution'. True, the bulk of Vaillant's work is rich in detail and full of insights into the psychological dynamics of the participants, but this one table is sufficient to make the reader hesitant to accept his thesis in other respects. This is because it reveals a rating technique which employs highly questionable indicators.

Table 4.5 Some methods and views on the developmental process

Theorist	Sample	Method	Developmental process
Levinson (1978, 1986) Life cycle of men	• 40 men, 35–45 years in 1968–70. All American born. 10 biologists, 10 blue collar workers, 10 novelists, 10 business executives. • Social class: varied. • Race, ethnicity: mixture. • Education: 70% completed college. • Marital status: all had been married at least once.	• Biographical interviewing 10–20 hours each. • Test as part of interview. • Task was to construct the 'story' of each man's life. • Interview protocols provided basis for generalisations about the life cycle.	• Building and modifying life structures (basic pattern of a person's life). • Alternation of stable and transitional periods in life structure. • Individualisation proceeds throughout the course of life – this refers to the relationship between self and the external world.
Gould (1972, 1978, 1990) Stages in the development of adult consciousness	• 125 psychiatric residents. • Unspecified number of psychiatric out-patients. • Non-patients, 524, 16–50 years, white and middle-class men and women.	• Cross-sectional. • Questionnaire and therapeutic observations. • Questionnaire contained statements based on expressed concerns of psychiatric patients: 160 questions on 10 areas of life – each area requiring a forced ranking of statements according to personal applicability (self-rating).	• People strive for a fuller more independent adult consciousness. • Growth implies reformulating our self definition and overcoming childhood consciousness. • Growth implies shedding the unconscious and restrictive set of protective devices which form the safety boundary of childhood, i.e. overcoming major false assumptions.

Lowenthal et al. (1977)
Four stages of life
	• 216 urban men and women, largely Caucasian, middle and lower-middle class.
	• Four groups:
	  High School mean age 17
	  Newlywed " " 24
	  Middle aged " " 50
	  Pre-retirement " " 60
		• Cross-sectional.
		• Interviews (8 hours):
		 – Structural interview schedule and
		 – measures and rating related to adaptation.
			• No global theoretical framework – but uses a range of theoretical concepts to understand adaptive processes across the lifespan, e.g. complexity, expressiveness, self-image, life satisfaction, perspectives on past and future, perceived stress, perceptions of continuity in value structure.

Chickering and Havighurst (1981) Adult developmental tasks	No direct research reported.	Relies on a range of developmental phase studies.	Three sources of developmental tasks: 1 physical/biological 2 social/cultural life 3 personal values and aspirations of the individual
Loevinger (1976) Ego development	A number of studies using undergraduate students.	• Systematic comparison of her stages with those of other stage theorists, e.g. Erikson, Fromm, Piaget, Sullivan, Kohlberg, Perry. • Projective tests requiring sentence completion (e.g. education is . . .)	• Ego is a central frame of reference for understanding self and others. • There is a developmental movement from simple stereotyped thinking and perceptions to a more complex and differentiated view of self and world.
Vaillant (1977, Vaillant and Vaillant 1990) Hierarchy of adaptive mechanisms	Initially 268 male undergraduates (1939–44). 94 male graduates followed up at regular intervals until 1987.	Longitudinal (Grant Study) interviews and annual questionnaires. Initially extensive physical, physiological and psychological examinations.	• Ego defence mechanisms mature through the life cycle – especially for those who were psychosocially mature in Erikson's sense.
Gilligan (1986) Women's development	21 women, 15–33 years, from diverse backgrounds.	Semi-structured interview.	Three levels of moral judgement: 1 Focus on self 2 Responsibility for self and others 3 Caring for others equated with the 'good' together with catering for individual needs under the moral principle of non-violence.

Table 4.6 Differences between best and worst life outcomes relevant to an Eriksonian model of the life cycle

	Best life outcomes (30 men) (%)	Worst life outcomes (30 men) (%)
Childhood environment poor	17	47
Pessimism, self-doubt, passivity and fear of sex at 50	3	50
In college personality integration put in bottom fifth	0	33
Subjects whose career choice reflected identification with father	60	27
Dominated by mother in adult life	0	40
Failure to marry by 30	3	37
Bleak friendship patterns by 50	0	57
Current job has little supervisory responsibility	20	93
Children admitted to father's college	47	10
Children's outcome described as good or excellent	66	23
Average yearly charitable contribution	$3,000	$500

Source: Vaillant (1977: 350; see also Vaillant and Vaillant 1990)

Conceptions of the healthy personality

Development implies growth and progress, not merely change. But growth and progress towards what end? The answer to this question is often the starting point for theories of adult development, and it is the conception of the end point of development, the 'mature' or 'healthy' personality, which frequently governs how progress and growth is monitored and explained within a given theory. For Kohlberg, growth is towards autonomous and principled morality, for Erikson, towards inner unity, and for Maslow, it is towards self-actualisation with its increased sense of self and autonomy. Many developmental psychologists construe the end point of development with terms like 'individuality', 'autonomy' and the 'integrated self'.

But do such descriptions represent a particular way of looking at the world which excludes certain cultures or sections of the population? A closer look may help to resolve this issue. Levinson (1978), for example, makes the following remarks about the 'individuation' process:

> Throughout the life cycle, but especially in the key transition periods such as infancy, pubescence and the Mid-life Transition, the developmental process of individuation is going on. This term refers to the changes in a person's relationship to himself [*sic*] and to the external world. The infant, leaving his mother's womb, must gain some idea of his separate existence. He must decide where he stops and where the world begins. He must separate himself from his mother, yet maintain

a tie to her. He must form a sense of 'reality' that allows him to accept his surroundings as having an independent existence not necessarily subject to his control. The child's world gradually expands to include his family, neighborhood and friends; and his self becomes more complex through his relationships with other persons and institutions.

These changes are part of the individuation process. In successive periods of development, as this process goes on, the person forms a clearer boundary between self and world. He forms a stronger sense of who he is and what he wants, and a more realistic, sophisticated view of the world: what it is like, what if offers him and demands from him. Greater individuation allows him to be more separate from the world, to be more independent and self-generating. But it also gives him the confidence and understanding to have more intense attachments in the world and to feel more fully a part of it.

(Levinson 1978: 195)

This emphasis on 'separateness', 'independence' and 'self-generation' is the language of the ethic of individualism, which receives attention elsewhere in this book. For the present it is worthwhile noting the claims of at least one commentator, Gilligan (1986), that the emphasis on the development of individual identity among developmental theories is an aspect of gender bias which pervades the literature. She begins her analysis by referring to the work of Chodorow (1978), who observes that, in general, girls are parented by a person of the same gender while boys are parented by a person of the opposite gender. The significance of this is that the identity of boys is built on the perception of contrast and separateness from their primary caregiver, while the identity of girls is built upon the perception of sameness and attachment to their primary caregiver. Gilligan remarks:

Consequently, relationships, and particularly issues of dependency, are experienced differently by women and men. For boys and men, separation and individuation are critically tied to gender identity since separation from the mother is essential for the development of masculinity. For girls and women, issues of femininity or feminine identity do not depend on the achievement of separation from the mother or on the progress of individuation. Since masculinity is defined through separation while femininity is defined through attachment, male gender identity is threatened by intimacy while female gender identity is threatened by separation. Thus males tend to have difficulty with relationships, while females tend to have problems with individuation. The quality of embeddedness in social interaction and personal relationships that characterizes women's lives in contrast to men's, however, becomes not only a descriptive difference but also a developmental liability when the milestones of childhood and adolescent development in the psychological literature are markers of increasing separation. Women's failure to separate then becomes by definition a failure to develop.

(Gilligan 1986: 8–9)

Gilligan then proceeds to cite evidence of the undervaluing of female characteristics – the concern with relationships and responsibilities, empathy and attachment – among developmental theories. For example, Freud considered the persistence of women's pre-Oedipal attachment to their mother to be linked with their failure to resolve completely their Oedipal feelings and their consequent failure to develop a strong super-ego. This developmental failure in women results (in Freud's view) in their having little sense of justice:

> The fact that women must be regarded as having little sense of justice is no doubt related to the predominance of envy in their mental life.

(Freud 1973b: 168)

Another example comes from Jean Piaget, who observed sex differences in the way children engage in games. Girls, because of their more flexible attitude towards rules and their enforcement, were considered to have a less developed legal sense than boys – which is the cornerstone of moral development:

> [for boys and girls] the rule is no longer an imperative coming from an adult and accepted without discussion, it is a means of agreement resulting from co-operation itself. But girls are less explicit about this agreement and this is our reason for suspecting them of being less concerned with legal elaborations. A rule is good so long as the game repays it.

(Piaget 1977a: 78)

Kohlberg too is open to the same criticism. Gilligan observes that his empirical work, which led to the formulation of moral development stages, was based on a sample of boys only. Not surprisingly, women tend to score lower on Kohlberg's scale than men. According to Gilligan, this is because the higher stages of Kohlberg's scale are constructed from what are traditionally 'male' qualities – the concern with justice and rights (premised on individuation) rather than with responsibilities and relationships.

The thrust of Gilligan's argument is that womanhood is rarely equated with mature healthy adulthood in much of the adult developmental literature. This is because the healthy personality is too often portrayed from a male perspective, with an emphasis on individuation and autonomy.

The elusive mystery of women's development lies in its recognition of the continuing importance of attachment in the human life cycle. Woman's place in man's life cycle is to protect this recognition while the developmental litany intones the celebration of separation, autonomy, individuation, and natural rights.

(Gilligan 1986: 23)

The influential and much cited work *Women's Ways of Knowing: The Development of Self, Voice and Mind* (Belenky *et al.* 1986) supports Gilligan's position. The authors are concerned with the development of self and mind in women. The interviews reveal among women a valuing of engagement, subjectivity, dialogue and interaction in the way that they construe knowledge and depict their development. For women the development of 'voice' is the key to the development of mind and self. The authors identify five categories in the development of women's knowledge:

1 Silence: this is more a state of unknowing where women are mindless and voiceless.
2 Received knowledge: knowledge which is received from external authorities and reproduced without change by women.
3 Subjective knowledge: personal, private, experienced-based knowledge from within the individual woman.
4 Procedural knowledge: exterior, rational, so called 'objective' knowledge which predominates in many formal education systems.
5 Constructed knowledge: women are able to value both subjective and objective strategies as a means to contextual knowledge and moral conviction which they construct for themselves.

The ideal developmental outcome is to be able to integrate all the voices of knowledge: to acknowledge the violence and oppression of 'silence' at one end of the spectrum and to incorporate subjectivity and dialogue into a form of constructed knowledge at the other. This idea that women's ways of knowing are different from men's has found expression in feminist critiques of how knowledge is constructed and controlled in the formal study of adult education. In particular there has been a challenge to the idea of objective, neutral research; and an analysis of institutional structures and power relations which disempower women and promote 'androcentricity' (see Stalker 1996 for a recent analysis).

Other empirical support for Gilligan's position can be found in studies which have aimed to validate Levinson's model using female subjects and in studies which have sought to identify the life cycle of women in their own right. Caffarella and Olsen (1993), in their review of over sixteen studies, provide a useful summary of the results. Generally the studies reviewed reconfirm the importance of interpersonal relationships in women's self concept, point to the difficulties experienced by women in balancing a multiplicity of roles, highlight the diversity and discontinuity of women's development, and note generational differences resulting from historical changes in opportunities and the availability of role models.

Given the conceptual and empirical difficulties in mapping developmental stages outlined above, perhaps it is best to abandon the project of identifying universal age-related stages or phases of development, and focus more on the process of change and transformation and how the various factors in development interact (i.e. biological, cultural, historical, psychological and physical).

DEVELOPMENT AS A DIALECTICAL PROCESS

An alternative to documenting the 'stages' and 'phases' of adult life is to understand development as an ongoing dialectical process (see Wozniak 1975; Riegel 1976; Buss 1979; Basseches 1984). The basic notion here is that there is a constant 'dialectic' between the changing or developing person and the changing or evolving society. That is, the person creates, and is created by the society in which he or she lives. Accompanying this notion is the rejection of those psychological approaches which search for stability, equilibrium and balance in the life course. The person is construed as a changing person in a changing world, and the dialectical approach is very much concerned with the dynamics of change:

> The preference for an equilibrium model in the behavioural sciences has been as firmly established as has the preference for abstract traits or competencies. Without any debate it has been taken for granted that a state of balance, stability and rest is more desirable than a state of upheaval, conflict and change. Thus we have always aimed for a psychology of satisfaction but not of excitement. This preference has found expression in balance theory, equilibrium theory, steady state theory, and indirectly in the theory of cognitive dissonance. With the possible exception of the latter, these interpretations fail to explore the fact that every change has to be explained by the process of imbalance which forms the basis for any movement. Once this prerequisite is recognized, stability appears as a transitory condition in the stream of ceaseless changes.
>
> (Riegel 1976: 690)

One source of such change is the historical change in one's culture (or subculture), the other source is the change associated with one's age-related social category (e.g. child's, youth, young adult, elder). Such changes are primarily mediated through people interacting in everyday life – thus an investigation of developmental change will entail an analysis of common, everyday interactions and the dialogues contained in them.

Riegel's position has much in common with Berger and Luckmann's (1967) exposition of how personal identity is shaped, maintained and transmitted within a given social order. Their analysis offers a powerful account of how personal identity is a social construction which, especially in a modern pluralistic society, is constantly open to change and transformation. What is meant by the proposition that personal identity is a social construction? Put simply, the idea is as follows:

1 We do not have biologically determined identities.
2 We are all born into a particular social world which has been constructed by humans.
3 We develop a notion of who we are from the way 'significant' others (e.g. parents) treat us (interact with us).
4 These 'significant' others represent the social world and mediate it to us.
5 We take on the roles and attitudes of significant others, internalise them and make them our own.
6 We extend our identification with significant others to an identification with society as a whole: 'Only by virtue of this generalised identification does his own self-identification attain stability and continuity. He now has not only an identity vis-à-vis this or that significant other, but an identity in general.'

(Berger and Luckmann 1967: 153)

Identity, as a social construction, needs to be maintained through social interaction. The routines of everyday life serve to confirm the reality of the world and our place in it. In particular, the language used in everyday conversations confirms for us the silent, taken-for-granted world that forms the foundation of our personal identity. In modern pluralistic society, however, there is a multiplicity of world views or realities. Because there is no common social reality there is (after primary socialisation) no socially produced stable structure of personal identity. This means that achieving a stable personal identity in modern society becomes an individual, private enterprise. Moreover, the possibility of transforming one's identity is always present. Indeed, one could argue that many life events require a change or re-orientation of identity (e.g. retirement, caring for children, the death of a spouse).

Berger and Luckmann (1967) maintain that any transformation of identity requires a process of resocialisation. In extreme cases, such as with religious conversion, there may be a complete dismantling of one's former identity. This would require the following:

1 Affiliation with the new community;
2 Segregation of the individual from the inhabitants of other 'worlds', especially those from the 'world' being left behind (at least at the initial stages);

3 A reinterpretation of the old 'reality' in terms of the new 'reality' (e.g. Now I understand the purpose of my doing such and such).

Each of these steps can be recognised as an extreme version of what happens to many adults as they develop new personal, family, work and leisure pursuits. The difference between this analysis and the life span development literature is that transformation does not imply a move towards some state of maturity; it simply means change, not improvement. Also, there are no propositions about the regularity and predictability of change – only that personal identity is open to change, subject to the existence of a community of others who maintain the change through discourse in everyday life. But the view that development is a social construct need not entirely eliminate individual agency. This is particularly so with socially constructed age categories. Age category, unlike gender, is a continuum rather than a bipolar category. That is, individuals move from one category to another over time, which is not the case with gender. Thus one's positioning in an age category is tentative, and the boundaries of role appropriate behaviour are more fluid, uncertain and ambiguous. Perhaps this is why we are witnessing a breakdown in the predictability of the various phases and stages of development.

The idea of the malleability of personal identity is both a source of hope and an occasion for despair. Hope, because it means that change is always possible; despair, because it implies that a belief in the real, true, authentic self is a fanciful indulgence.

The studies cited in this chapter represent only a sampling of a rich and diverse field of inquiry. They were chosen to reveal some of the pitfalls in theory and research in adult development. Adult development is, in principle, germane to anyone with an interest in adult education. Too often, however, people with an applied intent will latch on to an easily assimilated theory, one which clearly differentiates and orders the 'phases' or 'stages' of life and which advances an unambiguous account of the process and end point of development. Adult educators may find such theories useful but they need to be wary of the methodological and conceptual difficulties. They also need to be mindful of the impact such theories have on shaping and maintaining conventionally held views about what it means to be a mature, healthy adult.

Chapter 5

The development of intelligence and cognition

An interest in adult learning invariably leads to a desire to understand cognitive changes during adulthood. In seeking to satisfy this desire, the adult educator is likely to encounter different models of cognitive development after maturity. One model, the 'stability' model, assumes that adult cognition remains essentially stable after maturity. The result of cognitive progress during childhood is the attainment of mature forms of reasoning and thinking which are then applied throughout the adult years. By contrast, the 'decrement' model postulates that there is a gradual decrease in the ageing individual's capacity to utilise and organise information, presumably the result of some kind of biological deterioration. Finally, the 'decrement with compensation' model, while accepting the notion of biological deterioration, also emphasises the compensatory effects of accumulated experience during adult life (Labouvie-Vief 1977).

The 'decrement' and 'decrement plus compensation' models are based on research deriving from a particular tradition in psychology – psychometric theory and methodology – which focuses on testing and measuring intellectual abilities. One of the most influential theories in this tradition is that proposed by Horn and Cattell (1967, 1968). They separate intellectual ability into two general factors labelled 'fluid' and 'crystallised' intelligence. Fluid intelligence is measured by tests of complex reasoning, memory and figural relations – tests which are said to be 'culture' fair and thereby linked with universal, biological development. Crystallised intelligence is measured by tests on information storage, verbal comprehension and numerical reasoning – those sorts of abilities which are normally associated with experience and acculturation. Horn and Cattell's research reveals that from the teenage years onwards, there is a decrease in fluid intelligence and an increase in crystallised intelligence. The net result is that intellectual functioning remains relatively stable with age; there is simply a shift in the balance between fluid and crystallised intelligence.

In the psychometric tradition, much of the debate about adult intellectual capacity has centred on how to measure and/or interpret the consistent finding that there is decline with age in performance on 'fluid' type psychometric tests. This is partly a methodological problem. Schaie and his colleagues have since addressed this with the use of studies which control for age, cohort (year of birth) and time-of-measurement effects (the year the tests were administered). In a twenty-one-year study, comprising a number of independent cross-sectional studies, Schaie (1983b) reports that intelligence does decline with chronological age, but not until relatively later in life. In the Primary Mental Abilities test, *verbal meaning* increases until age 63, *space* peaks at 46, and *reasoning* declines only after age 60. Moreover, where decline is found, it can normally be reversed through training (Schaie and Willis 1986). Even though the results of such studies offer a much more optimistic view of adult intellectual capacity, commentators such as Labouvie-Vief (1977, 1980) have long argued that we need to reconceptualise what we mean by 'intelligence' in its broader sense of 'adaptability' and that it is a mistake to think of intelligence along a single quantitative dimension where there is no distinction between how we measure the intelligence and adaptability of different age groups.

There have since emerged a number of studies on practical intelligence, and the development of expertise, or even wisdom, as positive aspects of ageing. For example, Sternberg (1990b) points to the differences between academic and everyday problem solving as a key to understanding adult intelligence. Everyday problem solving requires the ability to recognise and define problems; there is often no single correct answer and yet a choice must be made, the information available is incomplete, ambiguous or conflicting; the entire context has to be taken into account, and there is only partial feedback on performance. These circumstances are very different from those that pertain in typical intelligence tests, but they are the conditions under which adults act in workplaces, family and community life. Scribner (1986) confirmed some of these claims in her studies of the problem-solving strategies of experts and novices working in milk-processing plants. Chi *et al.* (1988) provide a useful summary of the results of research comparing experts with novices. The common factors associated with expertise are that experts excel mainly in their own domains, perceive large meaningful patterns in their domains, are faster and more economical, have superior memory, see and represent problems in their domain at a deeper level than novices, spend a great deal of time analysing a problem qualitatively, and have strong self-monitoring skills. This research on expertise is significant because it locates adult development firmly in the experiences of the adult and thereby raises questions about how experience can be effectively utilised for learning. But it does not address sufficiently the process by which expertise is acquired: is the process of becoming an expert generic or domain specific? Can one learn-to-learn from experience in the same way that one is capable of learning how to learn in an academic context?

It is at this point that the significance of Piaget's work becomes apparent. He supplies us with an alternative conception of cognitive growth, one which places the emphasis on qualitative rather than quantitative change and which focuses as much on the processes of growth as on the outcomes. Thus he challenges the view that children are simply quantitatively diminished adults: he claims that children progress through different *types* of thinking as they develop towards mature adult thought. Unfortunately Piaget does not provide us with an account of cognitive development past the adolescent years. Nevertheless his approach to childhood cognitive development can be used as a point of reference for illuminating the state of things in adulthood. In his description of cognitive development, Piaget postulates a number of stages through which the person progresses in an invariant sequence. These stages represent qualitatively different ways of making sense, understanding and constructing a knowledge of the world. Piaget is particularly concerned with documenting the development of a specific type of knowledge – the kind of knowledge which arises from acting in the world and reflecting on our actions and experiences. The following anecdote illustrates what Piaget has in mind:

> One of my friends who is a great mathematician described to me an experience that he had as a child. While counting some pebbles, he arranged them in a line, counted them from left to right, and found that there were ten. He decided to count them from right to left and found there were still ten. He was surprised and delighted, so he changed the shape again. He put them in a circle, counted around the circle, and found there were still ten. . . . It was a great intellectual experience for him. He had discovered that the sum ten is independent of the order of counting. But unlike their weight, neither the sum nor the order is a property of the pebbles. The sum and the order come from the actions of the subject himself. It was he who introduced the order and it was he who did the counting. So logico-mathematical experience is experience in which the information comes from the subject's own actions and from the coordinations among his actions.
>
> (Piaget 1977b: 6–7)

It is the emergence of this type of knowledge in the person, logico-mathematical knowledge, that Piaget documents and orders into a sequence of stages, labelled sensory-motor (approx. 0–2 years), pre-operational (approx. 2–6 years), concrete-operational (approx. 7–11 years) and formal-operational (12 years plus). These stages represent qualitatively different ways of making sense, understanding and constructing a knowledge of the world. For example, the earliest stage is characterised by a practical intelligence where the infant learns to act in the world and produce effects. Innate reflexes such as grasping and sucking form the basis of a few rudimentary action patterns that the infant develops. Eventually these action patterns become co-ordinated so that objects which are seen may then be reached for, grasped, brought to the mouth and sucked. Literally, the world is a place to be grasped and sucked, it is a world of sensations and there is no differentiation between the self, the objects encountered, and one's actions on those objects. Indeed the world and its objects have a reality only if they can be sensed. During this stage these distinctions are gradually acquired and the infant comes to understand that objects have an independent existence. In the pre-operational stage the child can think about objects and events when they are absent. This capacity for representational thought is the foundation for deferred imitation (imitating a person's actions after some time has elapsed), make believe (pretending to do and be various things) and language. Despite these advances, the stage is best characterised by the limitations of the child's thought processes, such as the inability to take the role or view of the other person (egocentrism), the tendency to focus on only one aspect of an object or event when reasoning (centration), the tendency to endow inanimate objects with human qualities (animism) and the propensity to link ideas and things through association only (intuitive thought). In the concrete-operational stage the child has a more coherent and integrated cognitive system which permits an understanding of concepts (such as quantity, length, number, weight, volume) and an understanding of classes and their relationships.

It is the final stage which marks the commencement of mature adult thought. The distinctive mark of the formal-operational child is the capacity to think hypothetically about the 'possible', that is, to think in abstract terms. This is the basis of logical, scientific thinking, but it also leads to an understanding of abstract principles enshrined in the social order (e.g. justice, ethics, moral philosophy). The two experiments outlined in Table 5.1 illustrate some of these capacities.

In the balance beam experiment, the concrete-operational child fails to see how distance systematically compensates for weight and how weight systematically compensates for distance. The child understands the influence of weight and distance alone, but cannot co-ordinate the two. In the chemical solutions experiment, the formal-operational child can systematically list all possible combinations and thus be guaranteed of finding the solution. By contrast, the concrete-operational child can systematically test the simple combinations – but any further attempts are based only on trial and error. The performance of the concrete-operational child is limited by his or her cognitive structure.

There are some propositions in Piaget's theory which trigger the interest of adult educators. First, his outline of the principal stages of cognitive development immediately raises questions concerning the meaning of

Table 5.1 Comparison of concrete operations and formal operations on two tasks

Material	Task	Concrete operations	Formal operations
Balance beam			

| Chemical solutions filled with colourless, odourless liquids | To produce the colour yellow, knowing that g + one of, or some combination of 1, 2, 3 and 4 will produce yellow | $1 + g$ $2 + g$ $3 + g$ and some haphazard complex combinations e.g. $1 + 4 + g$ $2 + 3 + g$ | Systematically tests all possible combinations until the solution is found |

'stage' and the relationship between different stages. This is an inquiry worth pursuing because it has relevance for the entire gamut of stage developmental theories. Second, his description of the processes which account for development from one stage to the next has implications for our understanding of learning in a more general sense. Finally, his conception of mature adult thought (formal operations) challenges the idea of fundamental cognitive developmental progress during adulthood.

THE MEANING OF 'STAGES' AND THEIR RELATIONSHIPS

Flavell (1971, 1972) has completed a thorough analysis of the problems and issues in describing development in terms of a sequence of stages. But first, Flavell and Wohlwill provide us with a crisp definition of 'stage'.

> Most typically, the stage concept is invoked to refer to a mode, pattern, or constellation of behaviours for dispositions towards behaviour that seems to characterize some definable period in the child's life, be this period specified in terms of chronological age (with the resultant difficulty of taking individual differences in rate of development into account) or in terms of its position in a sequence. The expression 'the stage of infancy' would exemplify the former, while 'the crawling stage' would illustrate the latter use.
>
> (Flavell and Wohlwill 1969: 91)

One of the first issues in identifying a stage concerned the range of behaviours that it should encompass. In the above definition the 'crawling stage' is quite narrow and specific, while the 'stage of infancy' is general and non-specific. Narrowly defined, purely descriptive stages risk the charge of being of little interest theoretically, whereas stages which have a high degree of generality are thereby invested with a theoretical status beyond the purely descriptive. The Freudian stages, mentioned earlier, have a high degree of generality, and they serve to unite quite disparate and seemingly unrelated behaviours. Indeed, this unifying aspect is a characteristic of Piaget's theory and it is arguably a necessary condition for the concept of stage to be at all meaningful. Flavell outlines four components of the stage concept:

1 Qualitative changes – 'Stage to stage development entails qualitative rather than quantitative changes in thinking' (Flavell 1971: 423).
There are many quantitative changes in development but it would be ludicrous to label them stages (e.g. the 'counting to ten stage' as opposed to the 'counting to twenty stage' or the '100 word vocabulary stage' as opposed to the '2,000 word vocabulary stage'). Quantitative changes describe 'less' and 'more' of a particular ability whereas qualitative changes describe a shift to a different type of ability.

2 Abruptness – 'The development of individual stage specific abilities is characteristically abrupt rather than gradual' (Flavell 1971: 425).
This 'abruptness' criterion raises the issue of whether there is an increase in the functional maturity of an ability within a particular stage (i.e. does the ability develop from an initial level of competence to a more advanced level?). This is an important issue because it determines whether a stage is conceived of as a 'state' or as a 'process'. For Piaget a 'stage' has both these elements: 'A stage thus comprises both a level of preparation, on the one hand, and of achievement on the other' (Piaget 1955: 35, quoted in Flavell 1971: 428).

3 Concurrence – 'The abilities which define a particular stage develop concurrently, i.e. in synchrony with one another' (Flavell 1971: 435).
The notion of concurrence is quite slippery because once the acquisition of an ability is regarded as an extended process it becomes difficult to know what concurrence means. It could mean two abilities commencing at the same time but 'maturing' at different times. Or it could mean two abilities commencing at different times but maturing at the same time.
Whichever of these is the case, there are insurmountable problems in measuring 'concurrence' and the evidence that exists does not seem to support the idea of a tight synchrony in the development of different abilities. In addition, Flavell argues that concurrence is not essential to the stage concept: 'Surely the fact that these items are now functionally interrelated in your head, now comprise a tightly knit cognitive structure, etc., in no way implies that you must have acquired them all simultaneously' (Flavell 1971: 442).

4 Structures – 'Stage specific abilities become organised and interrelated to form cognitive structures' (Flavell 1971: 443).
At its most simple level, a structure will consist of two or more abilities that are interrelated. In addition, these abilities and their relationships are relatively stable and form the underlying basis of a range of superficially distinct behaviours (e.g. the rules we use to construct sentences). Flavell (1971) argues that it is difficult to contest the existence of cognitive structures – cognitive abilities characteristically interact in various ways to form total concepts. The more important issue is not whether 'cognitive structures' exist but how to verify or falsify particular structures.

If we set aside for the moment the problems and issues associated with 'stages' and their measurement, there remains the need to specify the kinds of relationships that exist between different stages. Many developmental theories postulate a *sequence* of stages, but for a particular sequence to be theoretically interesting the relationship would need to be more than merely temporal. What are the principal ways in which stages may be related? Flavell (1972) documents five such relationships:

1 Addition, i.e. later stages add to earlier stages.
2 Substitution, i.e. later stages replace earlier stages.
3 Modification, i.e. later stages are modified or more advanced versions of earlier stages.
4 Inclusion, i.e. earlier stages form a subset of later stages – they are a logical prerequisite of later stages.
5 Mediation, i.e. the earlier stage is a bridge to the development of a later stage.

DEVELOPMENTAL PROCESSES

In explaining the processes of cognitive development Piaget proposes certain mechanisms which are common to all stages. These mechanisms, or, as Piaget refers to them, 'functional invariants' (Piaget 1973: 62–3), derive from our biological make-up. One such functional invariant is organisation, which is the tendency to systematise, co-ordinate or structure the experience of objects in order to make such experience meaningful. Constructing 'cognitive structures' is thus a basic tendency of the organism. The other 'functional invariant' is adaptation, which consists of the two processes of assimilation and accommodation.

Assimilation is the tendency to distort or alter our encounters with new objects and experiences so that they fit within our existing understanding of the world (i.e. our cognitive structure). For example, the grasping reflex of the infant will be applied indiscriminately to a range of objects: large, small, thick, thin, soft and hard. This represents the infant's attempt to assimilate the objects of the world to its existing way of understanding the world. Certain objects may be actually physically amenable to such distortion (e.g. plasticine), but most are not. The world has a way of imposing its reality upon us and we are bound to 'accommodate' this reality. Accommodation is the tendency to alter our cognitive structures to fit the objects we encounter. The infant will thus begin to differentiate between different types of objects and the initial primitive grasp will be replaced by one which is more complex and more effective in manipulating objects.

The principle in this example extends to what are considered to be more 'cognitive' acts of the person: such as forming concepts, developing an understanding of rules or constructing strategies for solving problems. The principle is that the growth of knowledge is based on the interplay between assimilation and accommodation, between the person acting on and 'constructing' the world and the world acting on the person. In this way cognitive structures are formed, which essentially are a coherent set of strategies or rules which are used to understand the world.

In Piaget's account of development, these cognitive structures (which can be described in logico-mathematical terms) may be relatively stable and enduring affairs. That is, the person can apply them to make sense of the world, consistently and without contradiction. When this occurs the cognitive structures are said to be in equilibrium. However, Piaget asserts that some forms of equilibrium are 'superior' to others and that cognitive development proceeds from 'less' to 'more' adequate states of equilibrium. These states of equilibrium constitute the 'stages' of cognitive development previously outlined.

At this point Piaget needs to explain how and why the child moves from lower to higher equilibrium states. In order to do this he incorporates into his system a process which reflects a basic motivational factor in development; he refers to the process as equilibration. In its motivational aspect it refers to a search for better equilibrium, which is a tendency inherent in all healthy organisms. Rotman remarks:

> the need for this balance arises endogenously, it is imposed on an individual from within rather than from any source in society, and its satisfaction is a biological necessity essential to the health and well being of the organism. Indeed, for Piaget durable disequilibria constitute pathological organic or mental states.
>
> (Rotman 1977: 96)

Thus not only is there an intrinsic need for schemes or cognitive structures to function but also they seek to function at the highest possible level of equilibrium. Lower level equilibrium states are indeed a kind of disequilibrium state in that they are 'equilibrated' only with respect to a limited field of application. Any attempt to extend the field of application

will lead to conflicting and competing subschemes; the child will encounter inconsistency and contradiction in his or her experience which will
ultimately be resolved by a reorganisation of the child's cognitive structure
at a higher level. This is the mechanistic aspect of equilibration: when
contradictions arise through the inadequacies of lower level equilibrium
states then cognitive progress will ensue.

An experiment of Doise and colleagues (1976) illustrates this process
quite nicely. They used a standard Piagetian test for the conservation of
length:

> A child who does not attain conservation of length admits that two equal
> rulers, whose ends perceptually coincide, are of equal length, but when
> one of the rulers is displaced so that one of its tips is no more in line
> with the tip of the other ruler, the non-conserving child thinks that one
> ruler is now longer than the other.
>
> (Doise *et al.* 1976: 245)

When children claim that, after a displacement, one ruler is longer than
the other, the typical adult correction is to say 'no, the top ruler is further
here, but the bottom ruler is further there, so both are the same length'.
However, Doise *et al.* (1976) show that a more effective intervention is to
point to the opposite end of the other ruler and say: 'I think this ruler is
longer, you see, it goes further there'. The ingenuity of this experiment is
that children were provided with a model of reasoning similar to their own
but which led to a different judgement. Presumably this highlighted the
contradictions inherent in their inability to conceive length, and the
perception of this contradiction acted as a springboard for cognitive
progress. Conflict and contradiction, then, lie at the heart of cognitive
development.

To sum up, Piaget's view of the development of knowledge is that
fundamentally invariant cognitive processes (organisation, assimilation,
accommodation, equilibration) progressively produce qualitatively different equilibrium states, or 'stages' through which the child passes in his
or her development towards adult forms of reasoning.

To reiterate, there are a number of ways in which Piaget's work is
relevant to an understanding of adult learning and development. His most
pertinent legacies in this respect are:

1 The emphasis on qualitative rather than quantitative developmental
   changes in cognition (and his related 'structuralist' approach to cognitive development).
2 The importance attached to the active role of the person in constructing
   his or her knowledge (with the implication that learning through
   activity is more meaningful).
3 A conception of mature, adult thought (i.e. formal operations).

Each of these legacies is apparent in research and theory which attempts to extend Piaget's work to the years beyond adolescence, and/or which applies his approach to different developmental domains (such as the development of morality, or social cognition). They are also apparent, however, as focal points in the literature which offers a critical appraisal of his work.

CRITIQUE OF PIAGET

Piagetian theory has received a great deal of criticism on conceptual and methodological grounds. There are the usual charges that his 'experiments' are badly controlled and incompletely reported: that he fails to provide precise and clear details of his procedure, that he varies his procedure from subject to subject, that he omits rudimentary information about his subjects, and that he omits checks on the face validity and reliability of his stage classification procedures. In addition he is said to have a tendency to over-interpret his data and to leave large gaps between his theory construction and the empirical findings that he is writing about. Some of the conceptual difficulties of his theory are implicit in the foregoing analysis of the concepts of 'stage' and 'sequence'. It is apparent from this analysis that it is difficult, if not impossible, to establish empirically that two or more cognitive acquisitions do in fact emerge in a particular chronological order in an individual's life.

All the above criticisms deal with conceptual and methodological difficulties within the framework of Piaget's theory. Two important criticisms, however, strike at the core of his work. The first of these relates to a tension between two features of Piaget's theory – his structuralism and his constructivism. The second concerns the adequacy of formal operations as a complete account of mature, adult thought.

Piaget's 'structuralist' approach is exemplified by his description of a sequence of 'stable' cognitive structures in the course of development. His 'constructivist' approach is to be found in his explanation of the processes of cognitive development – processes which explain change rather than stability. The person, through interactions with the environment, constructs his or her knowledge through the interplay between assimilation and accommodation. Now the issue is whether structuralism or constructivism dominates in Piaget's work. There are two lines of argument which suggest that structuralism dominates. One of these is expressed by Basseches:

> while it is relatively easy to see how the constructivist model operates in Piaget's description of infants' cognition, it gets harder and harder as one moves up the developmental scale. More and more, assimilation seems to dominate over accommodation, so that finally we have clear

explanations and examples of how adolescents apply their formal operational structures to solving problems, but we have no such explanations or examples of how new experiences force adolescents to construct new forms of reasoning that transcend the limits of their formal analyses. The formal operational system seems so abstract that it can be applied to any kind of problem without accommodation.

(Basseches 1984: 52)

In Piaget's scheme of things there is no further structural change after the attainment of formal operations. Formal operational thought is a closed system structure which can assimilate any experience. According to Basseches, this implies that the dialectical interplay of assimilation and accommodation ends with formal operational thought – a view which he and others (Riegel 1973; Buck-Morss 1975) reject.

The Piagetian approach has been applied to the years beyond adolescence but the research has mainly focused on whether, and how, formal operational thought is generalised, extended and maintained in adulthood (see Long 1983 for a summary). Another line of inquiry has highlighted the limitations of formal operations in describing mature adult thought. A common thread in this inquiry is that mature adult cognition is characterised by the ability to fit abstract thinking into the concrete limitations of everyday life. Labouvie-Vief captures the spirit of this inquiry:

> While the theme of youth is flexibility, the hallmark of adulthood is commitment and responsibility. Careers must be started, intimacy bonds formed, children raised. In short, in a world of a multitude of logical possibilities, one course of action must be adopted. This conscious commitment to one pathway and the deliberate disregard of the logical choices may mark the onset of adult cognitive maturity. . . .
>
> The pure logic of youth may, of course, serve a local or temporary adaptive value, and therefore its importance should not be denigrated. It permits a circulatory exercise of operatory schemes that are to be put to pragmatic use later on. It thus helps to guarantee the flexibility demanded of mature adult adaptation. This is our first proposed conclusion: adulthood brings structural change, not just in the perfection of logic, but in its reintegration with pragmatic necessities.

(Labouvie-Vief 1980: 153)

This need to take into account pragmatic necessities may require the ability to tolerate contradiction and ambiguity, which, according to Riegel, is a feature of adult thought:

> The mature person needs to achieve a new apprehension and an effective use of contradictions in operations and thoughts. Contra-

dictions should no longer be regarded as deficiencies that have to be straightened out by formal thinking but, in a confirmative manner, as the very basis of all activities. In particular, they form the basis for any innovative and creative work. Adulthood and maturity represent the period in life during which the individual knowingly reappraises the role of formal, i.e. non contradictory thought and during which he may succeed again (as the young child has unknowingly succeeded in his 'primitive dialectic') to accept contradictions in his actions and thoughts ('scientific dialectic').

(Riegel 1975: 101)

In the above examples, formal operations is deemed to be limited by its abstractness and removal from everyday problem-posing and solving. It is a type of reasoning which is correctly applied to a very narrow range of problems, but which can play only a subordinate role in efforts to solve the concrete problems of adult life.

Piaget's emphasis on an invariant (and universal) sequence of stages leading to mature formal operational thought and his apparent disregard for psychological phenomena which defy structural analysis (feelings, beliefs, values, imagination, desire) has attracted a flood of what may be called 'ideology' critiques. This body of criticism is summarised and evaluated by Broughton (1981b) in the last of a series of five articles on Piaget's theory. Basically, Piaget's theory is portrayed as being an outgrowth of liberal ideology.

> The Piagetian developmental theory is criticized as a form of ideological legitimization which supports the current organization and political stratification of society and rationalizes the extant socialization processes reproducing the present social order, by showing them to be accurate reflections of 'natural', quasi-biological sequences of individual growth. From this critical perspective, both the sequence of structures and the theory of it represent purely *conventional* meaning systems, with no clear objectivity. The very concept of 'development' can even be construed as a reification of history deriving from the nineteenth century ideology of progress.

(Broughton 1981b: 387)

This is a forceful criticism but, on first encounter, it seems quite remote from Piaget's project. Nevertheless, it is possible to illustrate the validity and relevance of such a criticism by following the subsequent application of Piaget's theory to what is known as 'social cognition' – which encompasses the development of concepts of society, concepts of morality, concepts of politics, etc. By far the best known and often cited research in this area is that of Kohlberg on the development of moral judgement.

KOHLBERG'S RESEARCH ON MORAL JUDGEMENT

Kohlberg (1969, 1971, 1973) considers moral judgement to be a specific case of general cognitive development. His research technique is to present subjects with a moral dilemma, ask them to make a decision about the correct course of action, and then question them about the reasons for their decision. He is not concerned with the actual decisions or conclusions of the subjects, but with the way they reason about the moral issues involved (i.e. the structure of their moral reasoning). The standard moral judgement interview consists of three parallel forms. Each form comprises three hypothetical moral dilemmas followed by between nine and twelve standardised probe questions. The best known of these dilemmas is reproduced below.

> In Europe, a woman was near death from a special kind of cancer. There was one drug that the doctors thought might save her. It was a form of radium that a druggist in the same town had recently discovered. The drug was expensive to make, but the druggist was charging ten times what the drug cost him to make. He paid $400 for the radium and charged $4,000 for a small dose of the drug. The sick woman's husband, Heinz, went to everyone he knew to borrow the money, but he could only get together about $2,000, which is half of what it cost. He told the druggist that his wife was dying and asked him to sell it cheaper or let him pay later. The chemist said, 'No, I discovered the drug and I'm going to make money from it'. So having tried every legal means, Heinz gets desperate and considers breaking into the man's store to steal the drug for his wife.
>
> (Colby and Kohlberg 1987: 1)

The questions which follow in the interview include the following. Should Heinz steal the drug? Is it actually right or wrong for him to steal the drug? Does Heinz have a duty or obligation to steal the drug? Should Heinz steal the drug for a stranger? To reiterate, Kohlberg is not at all concerned with whether subjects believe Heinz should or should not have stolen the drug. The critical dimension is the reasoning the subjects use to justify their decision. Kohlberg (1969) found that the ability to reason about moral issues is acquired in the course of development and can be described in terms of a sequence of six stages, grouped into three levels (see Table 5.2). He claims that the relationship between the various stages of his 'sequence' of moral stages is similar to that postulated by Piaget in his cognitive developmental theory.

> A cognitive-developmental theory of moralisation holds that there is a sequence of moral stages for the same basic reasons that there are cognitive or logico-mathematical stages, that is because cognitive struc-

Table 5.2 Kohlberg's stages of moral development

Level	Stages
I Pre-conventional level At this level the child is responsive to cultural rules and labels of good and bad, right and wrong, but interprets these labels in terms of either the physical or hedonistic consequences of action (punishment, reward, exchange of favours), or in terms of the physical power of those who enunciate the rules and labels.	*Stage 1* The punishment and obedience orientation. The physical consequences of action determine its goodness or badness regardless of the human meaning or value of these consequences. Avoidance of punishment and unquestioning deference to power are valued in their own right, not in terms of respect for an underlying moral order supported by punishment and authority (the latter being stage 4). *Stage 2* The instrumental relativist orientation. Right action consists of that which instrumentally satisfies one's own needs and occasionally the needs of others. Human relations are viewed in terms like those of the market-place. Elements of fairness, or reciprocity, and of equal sharing are present, but they are always interpreted in a physical, pragmatic way. Reciprocity is a matter of 'you scratch my back and I'll scratch yours', not of loyalty, gratitude or justice.
II Conventional level At this level, maintaining the expectations of the individual's family, group or nation is perceived as valuable in its own right, regardless of immediate and obvious consequences. The attitude is not only one of conformity to personal expectations and social order, but also of loyalty to it, of actively maintaining, supporting and justifying the order, and of identifying with the persons or group involved in it.	*Stage 3* The interpersonal concordance or 'good boy–nice girl' orientation. Good behaviour is that which pleases or helps others and is approved by them. There is much conformity to stereotypical images of what is majority or 'natural' behaviour. Behaviour is frequently judged by intention: 'he means well' becomes important for the first time. One earns approval by being 'nice'. *Stage 4* The 'law and order' orientation. This is orientation towards authority, fixed rules and the maintenance of social order. Right behaviour consists of doing one's duty, showing respect for authority and maintaining the given social order for its own sake.

III Post-conventional, autonomous or principled level
At this level, there is a clear effort to define moral values and principles which have validity and application apart from the authority of the group or persons holding these principles, and apart from the individual's own identification with these groups.

Stage 5 The social-contract legalistic orientation, generally with utilitarian overtones. Right action tends to be defined in terms of general individual rights and standards which have been critically examined and agreed upon by the whole society. There is a clear awareness of the relativism of personal values and opinions and a corresponding emphasis upon procedural rules for reaching consensus. Aside from what is constitutionally and democratically agreed upon, right is a matter of personal 'values' and 'opinions'. The result is an emphasis upon the 'legal point of view', but with an emphasis upon the possibility of changing law in terms of rational considerations of social utility (rather than freezing it in terms of stage 4 'law and order'). Outside the legal realm, free agreement and contract is the binding element of obligation. This is the 'official' morality of the US government and constitution.

Stage 6 The universal ethical principle orientation. Right is defined by the decision of conscience in accord with self-chosen ethical principles appealing to logical comprehensiveness, universality and consistency. These principles are abstract and ethical (the Golden Rule, the categorical imperative); they are not concrete moral rules like the Ten Commandments. At heart, these are universal principles of justice, of the reciprocity and equality of human rights, and of respect for the dignity of human beings as individual persons.

Source: adapted from Kohlberg (1969)

tural reorganisations toward the more equilibrated occur in the course of interaction between the organism and the environment.

(Kohlberg 1971: 183)

Thus Kohlberg portrays his stages as representing a hierarchy of structures which become progressively more differentiated as development occurs. It is not appropriate here to provide an exhaustive account of the various criticisms of Kohlberg's theory. A dominant theme, however, is that Kohlberg does an injustice to the very concept of morality by treating it in such a formal and abstract way (Peters 1971; Buck-Morss 1975; Sullivan 1977; Morelli 1978; Youniss 1978; Habermas 1979; Henry 1980). For example, Sullivan (1977) argues that abstract formalisms are, in themselves, neither moral nor immoral, and that a fusion of the abstract and the concrete is necessary for moral commitment. In a similar line of argument, Peters (1971) contends that moral judgements cannot be said to be 'superior' without reference to some culturally specific value:

> A further point must be made, too, about any moral system in which justice is regarded as the fundamental principle: it cannot be applied without a view, deriving from considerations other than those of justice, about what is important. This point can be demonstrated only very briefly, but it is one of cardinal importance. When we talk about what is just or unjust, we are applying the formal principle of reason – that no distinctions should be made without relevant differences, either to questions of distribution, when we are concerned about the treatment which different people are to receive, or to commutative situations, when we are concerned not with comparisons but with questions of desert, as in punishment. In all such cases some criterion has to be produced by reference to which the X treatment is to be based on relevant considerations. There must therefore be some further evaluative premise in order to determine relevance. Without such a premise, no decisions can be made about what is just on any substantive issue. In determining, for instance, what a just wage is, relevant differences must be determined by reference to what people need, to what they contribute to the community, to the risk involved, and so on. To propose any such criteria involves evaluation.

(Peters 1971: 263–4)

Thus the 'highest' stage of moral development does not lead 'naturally' to justice, as Kohlberg would have us believe. This is because the concept of justice implies an act or a decision which is either just or unjust: it does not exist as an abstraction, unrelated to concrete action. The development of moral judgement involves more than progress in the purely contemplative awareness of different reasons for/against a course of action. For the term 'moral judgement' to have meaning, it must refer to values and beliefs and these are acquired through experiencing a *particular* socio-historical world. Some additional analysis is necessary, one which takes into account the way in which our feelings, beliefs, attitudes and values are shaped by forces outside the domain of cognition.

SITUATED LEARNING

Lave and Wenger (1991) provide a radical departure from traditional ways of conceiving learning and the development of knowledge with their concept of 'situated learning'. Although it is located outside the intellectual tradition of the literature on cognitive development, expertise or adult intelligence, it certainly addresses the issue of the role of context in the development of knowledge. For them the essential thing about learning is that it involves participation in communities of practice. At first this participation is peripheral (hence the term 'legitimate peripheral participation'), but it increases gradually in engagement and complexity until the learner becomes a full participant in the socio-cultural practices of the community (an 'old timer' rather than a 'newcomer'). They illustrate their view of learning with respect to five studies of apprenticeship: of Yucatec Mayan midwives in Mexico, of Vai and Gola tailors in Liberia, of US Navy quartermasters, of butchers in US supermarkets, and of non-drinking alcoholics in Alcoholics Anonymous. Theirs is truly a social theory of learning and this becomes evident as they articulate their assumptions about the person, the world, and their relations, and how they conceive of learning as social practice.

On a first reading of Lave and Wenger, it is tempting to locate their work firmly in a tradition which emphasises learning by doing, reflection on experience, and a decentring from the teacher to the learner. However, they are keen to distance themselves from this tradition, emphasising the view that learning is an 'integral and inseparable aspect of social practice' (Lave and Wenger 1991: 31). Their concept of situatedness is certainly very different from the notion of 'learning by doing' which is often construed as an approach to learning which is compatible with conventional forms of teaching, whereas being 'situated' means being engaged as a full cultural-historical participant in the world, where 'agent, activity, and the world mutually constitute each other' (p. 33). Learning by doing is often subsumed within processes of learning where practice is an integral part of learning, in a sense learning is situated in practice 'as if it were some independently reifiable process that just happened to be located somewhere' (p. 35). But Lave and Wenger stress again that learning is 'an integral part of generative social practice in the lived-in-world' (p. 35). Similarly, they claim that the idea of reflection on practice or action is misconstrued, because there is a difference between talking about practice from the outside and talking within it:

> In a community of practice, there are no special forms of discourse aimed at apprentices or crucial to their centripetal movement toward full participation that correspond to the marked genres of the question-answer-evaluation format of classroom teaching. . . . For newcomers then the purpose is not to learn *from* talk as a substitute for legitimate peripheral participation; it is to learn *to* talk as a key to legitimate peripheral participation.
>
> (Lave and Wenger 1991: 108–9)

The idea then of discourse about practice as somehow distanced from practice or standing outside it is alien to their analysis. Discourse itself is seen as a social and cultural practice and not a kind of second order representation of practice. Finally there is a paradoxical shift both *towards* and *away from* the learner in Lave and Wenger's analysis. The shift away from the learner is a product of their concern with focusing on the structure of social practice, so that learning is not so much a matter of individuals acquiring mastery over knowledge and processes of reasoning, it is a matter of co-participants engaging in a community of practice. The focus is thus on the community rather than the individual. Far from eclipsing the person, they claim the person in this community is a 'person-in-the-world', not an isolated individual, but a 'whole person' who is a member of a socio-cultural community. Theirs is a relational view of the person and learning.

Allied to this view of the learner is a rejection of the idea that learners acquire structures or schemata through which they understand the world. It is participation frameworks which have structure, not the mental representations of individuals. Learners can be characterised as having increasing access to participating roles in a community of practice.

> the skillful learner acquires something more like the ability to play various roles in various fields of participation. This would involve things other than schemata: ability to anticipate, a sense of what can feasibly occur within specified contexts . . . a prereflective grasp of complex situations . . . timing of actions relative to changing circumstances: the ability to improvise.
>
> (Lave and Wenger 1991: 20)

While participation in a community of practice is fundamentally concerned with the development of identity, it is not appropriate to speak of the internalisation of knowledge or the socio-cultural world of practice.

In contrast with learning as internalisation, learning as increasing participation in communities of practice concerns the whole person acting in the world.

(Lave and Wenger 1991: 49)

The person is defined by their relations within a community of practice; conventional views of internalisation, they argue, leave no scope for exploring the continuously evolving and renewed set of relations in this community of practice.

It is not surprising to find that Lave and Wenger reject the idea that knowledge can in any way be general, abstract or decontextualised. They argue that

> even so-called general knowledge only has power in specific circumstances ... abstract representations are meaningless unless they can be made specific to the situation at hand. ... Knowing a general rule by itself in no way ensures that any generality it may carry is enabled in the specific circumstances in which it is relevant. In this sense any 'power of abstraction' is thoroughly situated, in the lives of persons and in the culture that makes it possible.
>
> (Lave and Wenger 1991: 33–4)

Given that teaching is predicated on at least some degree of abstraction, decontextualisation and generality, Lave and Wenger's analysis has implications for how teaching and formal education are to be conceived. They presage such debate but do not engage in it, being content to note that, for the present, they are not concerned with an analysis of teaching, except to say that the relationship between teaching and learning is highly problematic, or, for their purposes, 'decoupled'. Indeed within situated learning, access to the expertise of 'old timers' or 'masters' is not conceived in asymmetrical terms of master–apprentice relations or the master as pedagogue, the focus instead being on the structuring of a community's learning resources.

Lave and Wenger are concerned with identifying the conditions which distort or enhance learning in communities of practice. For example, the prospects of learning from practice are diminished where there is conflict between newcomers and masters, bosses or managers; similarly learning is distorted when there are strong asymmetrical master–apprentice relationships. Legitimate peripheral participants need broad access to arenas of mature practice and they need fewer demands on their time, effort and responsibility for work than full participants. Finally, the socio-political organisation of practice needs to be 'transparent'; only in this way can learners develop as full participants:

> To become a full member of a community of practice requires access to a wide range of ongoing activity, old timers, and other members of the

community; and to information, resources, and opportunities for participation.

(Lave and Wenger 1991: 101)

In a later work Lave (1993) contrasts situated learning with what is presented as the limitations of traditional cognitive theory. These are four in number:

1 The assumed division between learning and other activity

> two theoretical claims that are in question here: One is that actors' relations with knowledge-in-activity are static and do not change except when subject to special periods of 'learning' or 'development'. The other is that institutional arrangements for inculcating knowledge are the necessary, special circumstances for learning, separate from everyday practices.

(Lave 1993: 12)

2 The focus on the transmission of new knowledge without addressing the invention of new knowledge in practice

> any simple assumption that *transmission* or *transfer* or *internalisation* are apt descriptors for the circulation of knowledge in society faces the difficulty that they imply uniformity of knowledge. They do not acknowledge the fundamental imprint of interested parties, multiple activities, and different goals and circumstances, on what constitutes 'knowing' on a given occasion or across a multitude of interrelated events.

(Lave 1993: 13)

3 The assumption of homogeneity of learning, learners and knowledge

> In contrast situated learning assumes heterogeneity. The heterogeneous, multifocal character of situated activity implies that conflict is a ubiquitous aspect of human existence. This follows if we assume that people in the same situation, people who are helping to constitute 'a situation' together, know different things and speak with different interests and experience from different social locations.

(Lave 1993: 15)

4 The portrayal of 'failure' as an individual inability or refusal to learn

> The idea of erroneous or mistaken understanding in a heterogeneous world takes on a new meaning as 'active normal social locations and practices' (Lave 1993: 16). How and when error is identified 'depends on whose socially positioned point of view is adopted, and on historically and socially situated conceptions of erroneous action and belief' (Lave 1993: 16).

The value of the work of Lave and others on situated learning is that they draw attention to the need to understand knowledge and learning in context, how new knowledge comes to be invented in practice, and how learning occurs through participation in a community of practice. In pursuing their project they make a number of claims which can certainly be contested. For example, the claim that in traditional cognitive theory there is a division between learning and everyday activity certainly cannot be sustained, at least with respect to cognitive structuralism, which also claims that activity is the source of knowledge. Similarly, to portray cognitive structuralism as being concerned only with the transfer of knowledge ignores its strong dialectical base, and to argue that internalisation assumes a kind of homogeneous world without conflict ignores the way in which the concept of internalisation specifically addresses the problem of conflict. But these criticisms do not necessarily detract from the main thrust of the situated learning project, which nevertheless does depend on at least two claims. First, that it makes no sense to talk of knowledge that is decontextualised, abstract or general, and second, that new knowledge and learning are properly conceived as being located in communities of practice. These two claims are examined below.

Lave (1993) argues that the 'contextual/decontextual' dualism is based on a view of context as a container, so that we speak of the 'context' in which a general rule applies more as an illustration of the general rule rather than an exploration of the context in its own right. This way of speaking places a greater value on decontextualised knowledge, it is something which is abstract and general which can be applied across a range of contexts (i.e. in a sense the context doesn't matter or it is trivial). This privileging of the general and the abstract over the particular and the practical is a pervading theme in the history of western culture and it has found expression in modern times in the way we measure achievement at school and, indeed, the way we measure the potential for achievement through the use of tests of intelligence and aptitude. The exploration of 'situated learning' rightly seeks to redress this imbalance and it is accompanied by parallel investigations into the nature of practical intelligence, expertise and tacit knowledge in the psychological literature. But Lave and others leave no scope for the idea that knowledge and learning can be decontextualised, and they reject the 'contextual/decontextual' dualism. This extreme position is perhaps the result of failing to make some distinctions which should be made. First, Lave and Wenger assume that something which is decontextualised is thereby 'abstract or general'. In many cases the motivation for learning is to be transported to a different time and space, to escape the 'situatedness' of one's life and enter into a previously unknown and unimaginable world. Camus (1995) captures the spirit of this type of learning in his de facto autobiography *The First Man*; here he is writing about how he (under the name of Jacques Cormery) and his childhood friend would devour library books as a stark contrast to the poverty in their daily lives:

> Actually the contents of these books mattered little. What did matter was what they first felt when they went into the library, where they would see not the walls of black books but multiplying horizons and expanses that, as soon as they crossed the doorstep, would take them away from the cramped life of the neighbourhood ... each book had its own smell. ... And each of these odours, even before he had begun reading, would transport Jacques to another world full of promises ... that was beginning even now to obscure the room where he was, to blot out the neighbourhood itself and its noises, the city, and the whole world.
>
> (Camus 1995: 193–4)

The point is that learning can occur which is seemingly unrelated to one's context or life situation, and in the above case this is precisely where the desire for learning was located. Also the learning being referred to is not necessarily more general or abstract, it is just different, and outside Camus's immediate experience of the world.

Second, Lave and Wenger seem to assume that the belief that knowledge can be decontextualised, general and abstract, leads to a view of the learning process as necessarily decontextualised, general and abstract. But their position on this point is a little uncertain:

> any power of abstraction is thoroughly situated, in the lives of persons and in the culture which makes it possible. On the other hand, the world carries its own structure so that specificity always implies generality.
>
> (Lave and Wenger 1991: 34)

Ironically this last sentence expresses quite nicely the spirit of cognitive structuralism. For example, in learning the concept of number, children manipulate and act on objects in a thoroughly 'situated' way. They may even learn to count these objects, but the ability to count does not constitute the acquisition of the concept of number: for this they need to recognise that the number of objects does not vary with how they are configured in space, or indeed what the objects actually are. In this scenario the abstract concept of number emerges from action in the world, and it is true that once this concept is attained, it is generally applied across contexts. With respect to the concept of number at least, the nature and configuration of objects is irrelevant – the nature of objects and their configuration may have different meanings in different contexts – but their number will remain invariant.

The second principal claim referred to above concerns the nature of learning in communities of practice. Although Lave and Wenger were conscious of the risk of romanticising communities of practice, in many respects they have done just this by omitting a range of questions and issues from their analysis. In their eagerness to debunk testing, formal education and formal accreditation, they do not analyse how their omission affects power relations, access, public knowledge and public accountability. Formal education and accreditation arguably provide points of access which would otherwise be denied to intending newcomers (especially in communities of practice dominated by a single sex, or race, or ethnic community, or age group) and this access forces changes on a community of practice outside those occurring through conflicts between newcomers and old timers. They also provide portability in the sense that access to geographically different communities of practice is ensured. While the balance of power between the academy and the professions may be critiqued for reproducing the social order, on the face of it, it is more 'world open' than a community of practice which contains within it the 'secrets' of practice which can be attained only through peripheral participation. There is also no analysis of how communities of practice respond to social and technological changes, where the newcomers, for example, may have knowledge and access to new technologies which will displace traditional methods of practice. Further, in their implicit critique of formal education, there is no recognition that many communitites of practice regard formal education as part of their 'practice' and that a condition of peripheral participation is that certain rites of passage (examinations) are passed. These rites of passage form part of the language of participation where learners learn *to talk* rather than *from talk* (any casual observation of the language of newcomers in a community of practice requiring a common qualification will confirm this).

The above comments are not intended to dissuade the reader from engaging with the concept of situated learning, but only to warn the reader that a full and uncritical acceptance of the analysis of Lave and others is not warranted. While it is important to understand the nature of learning in communities of practice, and how new knowledge is generated through practice, existing teaching and learning practices, with appropriate reforms, can accommodate the core ideas of situated learning . And in many respects it is adult education which is best placed to put situated learning into practice!

Chapter 6

Learning styles

'Cognitive style', 'learning style' and 'conceptual style' are related terms which refer to an individual's characteristic and consistent approach to organising and processing information. The idea that people have different learning styles is enticing for adult educators. First, it highlights the importance of learning processes (rather than teaching techniques), and it thereby raises questions concerning the ideal distribution of power and control among teachers and learners. Second, it is an egalitarian concept because it focuses on people's strengths and weaknesses so that the operative term describing learners becomes 'different' rather than 'bad', 'poor', 'average', 'good' and 'very good'.

There have been numerous attempts to classify the basic ways in which cognitive or learning styles differ. Messick and associates (1978) identify nineteen types of learning styles, each type being supported by a range of research articles and theoretical papers, and Smith (1984) tabulates seventeen learning style inventories. Squires (1981) observes that cognitive styles are typically represented as polar opposites of a single dimension so that a person is described as field dependent *or* independent, reflective *or* impulsive, serialist *or* holist, a converger *or* a diverger, and so on. These varied approaches to cognitive style should not be seen as mutually exclusive, rather they support the reasonable expectation that people differ in their learning styles in a number of ways. Because of this it would be naïve to expect that adult educators could systematically design and deliver a course to fit the learning style needs of their students. This chapter, in part, addresses the issue of how learning style information should be used in the adult classroom. However, this will be done in the context of describing and evaluating two dominant approaches to categorising cognitive styles, the field dependence/independence dimension identified by Witkin, and the Learning Style Inventory developed by Kolb and Fry.

FIELD DEPENDENCE AND FIELD INDEPENDENCE

The terms 'field dependence' and 'field independence' are associated with the programme of research triggered by Witkin's (1950) seminal report on individual differences in the influence of context in making simple perceptual judgements. He found that the perceptual judgements of some people are consistently influenced by context, while for others the context has little or no influence. In an early experiment he used a completely darkened room. All the subject could see was a luminous rod surrounded by a luminous square frame. Both the rod and frame could be independently tilted, clockwise or counter-clockwise, around a common focal point. The subject was required to adjust the rod so that it appeared vertical in the presence of a tilted surrounding frame (see Figure 6.1). Some people could do this quite accurately irrespective of the tilt of the surrounding frame (field independent people). Others adjusted the rod to 'vertical' by aligning it with the surrounding frame, even when the frame was tilted by as much as 30 degrees (field dependent people).

(a)   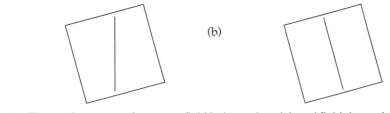   (b)

Figure 6.1 The performance of extreme field independent (a) and field dependent (b) subjects in Witkin's (1950) rod and frame test

In another version of this test, seated subjects were required to adjust their body to an upright position in a tilted room. Similar results were obtained: some subjects reported they were upright, when in fact they were tilted 30 degrees, while other subjects correctly adjusted themselves to the upright position without being influenced by the tilted room.

Witkin claims that these tests, and similar ones, measure a common factor: the ability to separate figure from context. He eventually developed a pencil and paper test, called the embedded figures test, designed to measure this general ability. In this test the subject is asked to locate a simple figure in a complex design. Once again some people find this task easy and complete it quickly (field independent), while others find it difficult and take longer to complete the test (field dependent). Witkin found a correlation between performance on the rod and frame and body adjustment tests. It is correlations such as these which led him to argue for the existence of different cognitive styles:

the common denominator underlying individual differences in performance in all these tasks is the extent to which a person is able to deal with a part of a field separately from the field as a whole, or the extent to which he is able to disembed items from organised context – to put it in everyday language, the extent to which he is analytical. At one extreme of the performance range, perception is strongly dominated by the prevailing field; we speak of this mode of perception as field dependent. At the other extreme, the perception of an item is relatively independent of the surrounding field, and we refer to this mode of perception as field independent.

(Witkin 1978: 42)

One may object that Witkin's tests measure an aspect of general intelligence and therefore add very little to our understanding of cognitive capacities. In this connection it is important to note that field independence/dependence does not represent a continuum from 'better to worse', as indicated by the observation that for some tasks the relatively field dependent person performs more accurately. However, there is some substance to this claim because of persistent evidence that field independent people perform better than field dependent people on *cognitive* tasks. Thus Witkin's cognitive style dimension is, at least, an ingredient of general intelligence; but it is much more than this, as demonstrated by numerous studies correlating field independence/dependence with a host of personal characteristics, social interaction patterns and life choices. The impact of these studies is that the concept of cognitive style has been extended from a narrow description of perceptual capacities to a more global description of different ways of knowing the world. For example, there are studies reporting how field dependent people rely on a social frame of reference to formulate their beliefs, attitudes and feelings, and self-concept; that they make fewer self-references in their speech; that they adapt their rate of speech to the rate of the person to whom they are communicating; that they are more sensitive to social cues; that they like to be with people; that they are better liked; that they prefer to be physically closer to others, and so forth. It is these associations with cognitive style that accounts for the interest of educators in the concept. Witkin *et al.* (1977) provided the first and most comprehensive analysis of the educational implications of cognitive styles. I have adapted and tabulated this analysis in Table 6.1. The table contains a summary of research findings which relate cognitive style to aspects of education; how students learn, how teachers teach, student–teacher interaction, and career and educational planning. On each of these aspects there is a difference between the strategies, choices and outcomes for field dependent and field independent people. For example, the table indicates how the process of learning is fundamentally different for people with different cognitive styles. Thus field dependent people are responsive to external reinforcement, they rely on externally provided structure, they focus on salient cues when identifying concepts, and they are better at learning and remembering social material. The sample of the research findings in the table has implications for teacher training, educational guidance and

Table 6.1 The educational implications of cognitive styles

	Field dependent	Field independent
How students learn		
1 Effect of reinforcement	External reinforcement more salient	Learn more under conditions of intrinsic motivation
2 Use of mediators in learning	Rely on externally provided structure, therefore need assistance with unorganised material	More likely to structure ambiguous material
3 Learning of concepts	Tend to focus on salient cues only – but their strategy can be altered with instruction	Tend to sample the entire array of cues (hypothesis testing approach)
4 Learning social material	Better at learning and remembering social material	Need assistance in focusing on social material
How teachers teach		
1 Methods	Prefer discussion method and situations which allow interactions with students	Prefer lecture and discovery methods, situations which are more impersonal and cognitive
2 Techniques	Avoid negative feedback and evaluation	Emphasise the need to correct errors and provide negative evaluation where appropriate
3 Teaching environment	Prefer rapport, participation, warm and personal environment	Show strength in the organisation and guidance of student learning
Education and career planning		
1 Educational/vocational interests, choices and achievements	Interpersonal domains which require social skills such as elementary school teaching, social sciences, rehabilitation counselling, welfare	Analytic and impersonal domains such as physical and biological sciences, mathematics, engineering, technical and mechanical activities
2 Interests and choices within educational/vocational areas	Favour specialisations with a 'people' emphasis, e.g. clinical psychology, psychiatric nursing, social studies teacher	Favour specialisations which are impersonal and require cognitive skills, e.g. experimental psychology, surgical nursing, natural science teaching
3 Making choices and changing areas	More undecided about occupational choice and less committed to their choice; shift their college majors away from impersonal and cognitive domains	Concerned with occupational planning, more specialised vocational interests; shift their college majors away from personal and social domains
Student–teacher interaction	When teachers and students are matched then: • they view one another more positively • teachers evaluate the performance and intellects of students higher • the goal of the interaction is more likely to be achieved The positive extremes of matching are the result of shared interests, shared personality characteristics, and shared modes of communication; teachers need to adapt their teaching strategies to the needs of dissimilar students	

counselling, learner induction, the streaming or grouping of students, and vocational preparation. But the implications are not clear cut and they depend on judgements of efficacy and value. Using the table as a guideline I will now address some of the issues in connecting educational practice with cognitive styles.

MALLEABILITY OF COGNITIVE STYLES

If cognitive styles are unalterable and there is a fixed relationship between cognitive styles and learning strategies, then there is little scope for helping learners overcome the limitations of their style. Fortunately, on first inspection, this does not seem to be the case. Witkin et al. (1977) review a number of studies which show that cognitive style, or at least its behavioural correlates, can be modified. For example, research indicates that the relative superiority of field dependent people in learning and remembering material with a social context is due principally to their selective attention to this material; field independent people do just as well when their attention is focused on such material. In a similar manner the relative inferiority of field dependent people in using hypothesis testing procedures in concept learning can be overcome by providing them with some simple directions on how to use this approach. Studies like these reveal that the impact of cognitive style on learning is modifiable. The implication for teachers is that they should be aware of learners' cognitive styles and apply corrective intervention where appropriate.

Witkin and his colleagues assert that individual differences in field dependence/independence are primarily due to socialisation. This suggests that they are, at least in principle, modifiable through education or training. However, an early longitudinal study (Witkin et al. 1967) illustrates the stability of cognitive style, especially during the period 17–24 years of age. Chickering is incredulous that this should be so:

> It is difficult for me to believe that change does not occur on the field dependence dimension during the college years and that such changes are not related to differences in college experiences and activities. . . . If no change occurred in field dependence and if no relationships to educational experiences and activities were found, it would mean that the field dependence versus independence characteristic has a stability among young adults that is not shared by several other similar variables.
> (Chickering 1978: 81)

This issue of the modifiability of cognitive style is likely to persist because it has implications for how best to provide advice and guidance to learners. If cognitive styles are stable and fixed then teaching intervention can be only cosmetic; under such circumstances it is best to adapt to the 'natural' inclinations of the learner (for example, attempt to match teaching and learning styles, develop alternative learning activities for people with different styles, guide people into those options to which they are suited). If, however, cognitive styles proved to be highly malleable then intervention can take a more active form (assist students to diversify their learning strategies, encourage optional choices outside a student's dominant style).

COGNITIVE STYLE AS A BIPOLAR DIMENSION

One attraction of a cognitive style approach is that it offers an alternative to the grading of student potential from 'better' to 'worse' along some quantitative dimension like intelligence. Intelligence is something one has 'more' or 'less' of, but this does not apply to cognitive style:

> the field-dependence-independence dimension is bipolar with regard to level, in the sense that it does not have clear 'high' and 'low' ends. Its bipolarity makes the dimension value-neutral, in the sense that each pole has qualities that are adaptive in particular circumstances.
>
> (Witkin and Goodenough 1981: 59)

The phrase 'adaptive in particular circumstances' is crucial here. It warns us that 'cognitive styles' are not to be read as different ways of acquiring the same kind of knowledge. Research indicates that different types of knowledge are 'more' or 'less' accessible to people with different cognitive styles. Table 6.1 indicates difference in the types of educational and vocational achievements associated with being field dependent/independent: field independent people do best with the analytical and impersonal domains such as the physical and biological sciences, mathematics, engineering, technical and mechanical activities; field dependent people do best with interpersonal domains requiring social skills, such as school teaching, the social sciences and welfare. But is there a status difference in the knowledge associated with these different domains and areas of work? I think that there is, and that in the current scheme of things field independence is valued more highly than field dependence. Field independence is associated with abstract and analytical thinking, which are important criteria for high status knowledge. It is also linked with better performance on tests of intelligence and other cognitive tests. Field independent people are said to structure ambiguous material more effectively and identify and form concepts more readily. To sum, the skills and qualities associated with field independence appear to be those that society at large values more highly (in this respect it is important to note that females are, at least marginally, more likely to be field dependent). Even in the arena of adult education, field independent people fare more favourably than field dependent people: they are more capable of dealing with a lack of clear direction (i.e. self-direction) and they learn more under conditions of intrinsic modification which Knowles claims is a feature of the adult as opposed to the child learner.

Thus the notion of cognitive style, in its field dependence/independence form, does little to liberate the learner from value judgements concerning worthwhile knowledge and worthwhile abilities. The position is exacerbated by the tendency to talk only of 'field independents' or 'field dependants' as if they were mutually exclusive and exhaustive categories into which all learners could be neatly sorted. This tendency is understandable because the dominant research technique is to make comparisons between the extremes of the bipolar dimension and thus document the limits of the differences between the two cognitive styles. But Witkin clearly indicates that the scores on tests of field independence/dependence form a continuous distribution. If this distribution is normal, then we would expect most people to have styles which reflect both field dependence *and* field independence. Given this, it is only a short step to acknowledging that in one context a person could be field dependent, and in another, field independent. This is the argument advanced by Wapner (1978):

> I maintain that [cognitive styles] are not independent of the context in which they operate and should not be defined as such . . . for example, there may be students who are more field dependent in the presence of an aggressive teacher and relatively less field dependent in the presence of a submissive teacher. To characterise people as occupying a *range* on the field dependence versus field independence dimension, with their manifest behaviour depending on the particular environmental context, involves a significant reconceptualisation.
>
> (Wapner 1978: 75–6)

This is a conceptualisation worth embracing because it is appropriate for the bulk of learners and it avoids the dangers associated with moulding cognitive style into an ideal typology.

MATCH/MIX-MATCH OF STYLES

Table 6.1 sets out some of the positive aspects of matching the styles of teachers and students. But Wapner (1978), quite rightly, challenges the educational benefits of matching cognitive styles:

> with a match in cognitive style there is a greater mutual attraction of student and teacher, greater communication through use of similar communication modes, and greater understanding and creation of a good atmosphere for learning. But is this the kind of environment that is optimal for learning? . . . Is an environment optimal if it conforms to the students' expectations? Is an environment optimal if the student

and teacher have understanding because they share similarity of view-point? A powerful argument can be made that opposition, contradiction and obstacles are necessary conditions for individual development and creativity.

(Wapner 1978: 77–8)

Wapner's comments are supported by the view, especially among cognitive developmental psychologists (see Doise 1978), that conflict is an important trigger for development. The argument is that the limitations of one's perspective become apparent only when opposing perspectives are encountered. Indeed, learning and development may be regarded as processes whereby initially alien experiences or contradictory observations become understandable through changes in the person. There are, of course, many claims and counter-claims regarding such a view, but most practitioners would agree that at least some unsettling experience is a good ingredient for effective learning. These considerations alone are sufficient to prevent one from rigorously matching cognitive styles, but there are two others worth mentioning. First, there is the question of whether matching cognitive styles, in any global sense, is at all possible. I argued in the immediately preceding section that the field dependence/independence dimension forms a continuous distribution and that most people occupy a range on that distribution. The upshot of this is that it makes no sense to try and 'match' the cognitive style of a teacher and a group of students: variations within the group and among the tasks set for the learners would pre-empt this. Second, there is the general question of whether education necessarily entails a broadening of the person. To what extent should educators demand that learners step outside the confines of their own skills and capacities and explore new ground? The argument here is that the person capable of learning a variety of things in different ways is better able to adapt to changed circumstances because they have learnt how to learn – which is often professed to be the most cherished outcome of the educational experience.

COGNITIVE STYLES AND ADULT LEARNING

Chickering (1978) illustrates how contract learning and programmed learning (which are both alternatives to traditional instruction and are associated with adult education) miss the target when it comes to cognitive styles. Neither of them is suited to one style or the other. Contract learning, for example, provides an opportunity for interaction (which suits field dependent people) but it is largely self-referent in the sense that the starting point for learning is the self (which poses difficulties for field dependent people). In a similar way programmed learning stresses impersonal, analytic skills (which suits field independent people) but its non-negotiable posture makes it difficult for those who have clearly defined personal goals (field independent). Having made these claims, Chickering then proceeds to offer what he regards as utopian solutions:

> The solution to contract learning lies simply in employing teachers who can distinguish the field-dependent student from the independent one and vary their teaching behaviours accordingly.... The problems presented by programmed learning are equally simple to solve. The answer lies in the direction of small modules at varying levels of complexity and comprehensiveness (i.e. to cater for choice).
>
> (Chickering 1978: 87–8)

The ideal adult teacher, then, is one who can diagnose learning styles and select, from an armoury of skills and techniques, the appropriate strategy for enhancing learning. It is a mistake to link a particular teaching method (such as contract learning) to a particular cognitive style. Each method can be implemented in a variety of ways which may or may not match the learner's style.

Given what has been said in the preceding discussion, the term 'diagnose' appears inappropriate for describing the role of the adult educator. It implies a privileged position which is (or should be) illusory. Ideally, learning styles should be on the agenda of any adult learning group, not as an instrument of the adult educator, but as an item for discussion and mutual scrutiny.

LEARNING STYLES AND THE EXPERIENTIAL LEARNING MODEL

Kolb and Fry (1975) and Kolb (1981, 1984) have developed an approach to classifying learning styles which is somewhat different from that of Witkin and his colleagues. The most important difference is that the learning styles they identify (Table 6.2) are closely linked to a model of the learning process, which is represented in Figure 6.2.

In this model, learning is conceived as a four stage cycle comprising an immediate concrete experience, observation and reflection on that experience, the formulation of an hypothesis or some kind of theory, and finally the testing of that theory through practical action. They argue that in any learning there is a conflict or tension between the polarities of at least two dimensions. The first of these dimensions has the concrete here-and-now experience at one pole, and abstract conceptualisation at the other. The second dimension has practical action and experimentation at one pole and detached reflective observation at the other. The ideal learner has the capacity to operate at either pole of both dimensions. Kolb and Fry (1975: 35–6) explain that learners, if they are to be effective, need four different kinds of abilities: concrete experience (CE) abilities, reflective

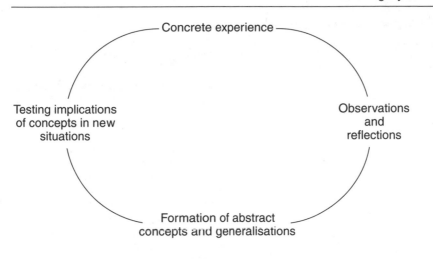

Figure 6.2 The experiential learning model

Source: Kolb and Fry (1975: 33)

observation (RO) abilities, abstract conceptualisation (AC) abilities and active experimentation (AE) abilities. That is, they must be able to involve themselves fully, openly and without bias in new experiences (CE), they must be able to reflect on and observe these experiences from many perspectives (RO), they must be able to create concepts that integrate their observations into logically sound theories (AC) and they must be able to use these theories to make decisions and solve problems (AE).

As it turns out, there are very few ideal learners, and most of us develop a preference or strength in one of the poles of each dimension. Kolb and Fry have developed a Learning Style Inventory (Kolb 1976), which is designed to measure a person's relative position on the 'concrete ex-perience' vs 'abstract conceptualisation' dimension and the 'active ex-perimentation' vs 'reflective observation' dimension. The inventory con-sists of lists of words which the respondent is asked to rank-order according to how best they describe his or her learning style. For example, if one chose the words 'analytical', 'thinking', 'logical', 'conceptualisation' and 'rational' in preference to 'receptive', 'feeling', 'accepting', 'intuitive', 'present-oriented' and 'experience', then a preference for abstract con-ceptualisation over concrete experience would be indicated. Using this procedure Kolb and Fry (1975) identified four basic learning styles, which are described in Table 6.2.

Many of the research findings, questions and issues raised in the immediately preceding section are pertinent to the learning styles described in Table 6.2. For example, there has been research linking these learning styles to vocational choices, professional socialisation, choice of

Table 6.2 Kolb and Fry's learning styles

Learning style	Learning characteristics	Description
Converger	Abstract conceptualisation + Active experimentation	• strong in the practical application of ideas • performs well when there is a single correct answers (e.g. IQ tests) • can focus hypothetical–deductive reasoning on specific problems • unemotional, prefers to deal with things rather than people • has narrow interests and chooses to specialise in the physical sciences • characteristic of many engineers
Diverger	Concrete experience + Reflective observation	• strong in imaginative ability • good at generating ideas and seeing things from different perspectives • interested in people • broad cultural interests • specialises in arts • characteristic of people with humanities and liberal arts backgrounds
Assimilator	Abstract conceptualisation + Reflective observation	• strong ability to create theoretical models • excels in inductive reasoning • concerned with abstract concepts rather than people – not too concerned with the practical use of theories • attracted to basic sciences and mathematics • often works in research and planning departments
Accommodator	Concrete experience + Active experimentation	• greatest strength is in doing things • more of a risk taker • performs well when required to quickly adapt to immediate circumstances • solves problems intuitively • relies on others for information • often found in action-oriented jobs such as marketing and sales

Source: adapted from Kolb and Fry (1975)

undergraduate majors, preference for different teaching methods and so on. Such issues as how best to alter one's dominant style, whether to match or mis-match teaching and learning styles, and how context influences one's style are relevant here in much the same way as in the discussion of field dependence/independence. To prevent repetition I will avoid any elaboration of these in the present context and instead comment on some of the unique aspects of Kolb and Fry's approach.

Like Witkin and his colleagues, Kolb and Fry challenge the notion that learning potential is reducible to a single dimension such as intelligence. Witkin showed us that there are at least two different but (ostensibly) equally valid ways of understanding the world. Similarly, Kolb and Fry argue, in opposition to received opinion, that the ability to think abstractly is no 'better' than the ability to be 'concrete'. But Kolb and Fry proceed one step further than Witkin when they acknowledge that each learning style has its strengths and weaknesses and therefore a person locked exclusively into one style is an incomplete learner. Becoming a 'complete' learner entails integrating the bipolar dimensions of each learning style, and operating comfortably in any learning style. They then proceed to link the notion of the 'complete' learner with a model of human development whereby a long period of accentuating one's dominant learning style (because of educational experiences and vocational choices) is followed by a capacity for integration (the reason for this is not clear). This should not be taken too seriously because it is not a model which is worked out in detail and there is no evidence offered in its support. I mention it only because it illustrates another attempt to connect the 'complete learner' with a utopian conception of psychological development.

Kolb and Fry, I think, are too extravagant in the significance they attach to their 'learning styles'. Even though the four learning styles are neatly constructed from dimensions which correspond to a model of the learning cycle, the model is not thereby validated. Clearly the model is not generalisable to all learning environments, different learning environments demand different learning styles (and Kolb and Fry cite this evidence) and there is no suggestion that it should be otherwise. What is then meant by the 'complete' learner? Is it someone who can adapt his or her learning style to any learning environment or is it someone who consistently applies an 'integrated' learning strategy to all learning environments? Kolb and Fry opt for the latter interpretation where the 'complete learner'

> is marked by increasing complexity and relativism in dealing with the world and one's experiences and by higher level integrations of the dialectical conflicts between the four primary adaptive modes – Concrete Experience, Reflective Observation, Abstract Conceptualisation and Active Experimentation.
>
> (Kolb and Fry 1975: 41)

Clearly they have in mind something much more grand than simply the ability to use whatever adaptive mode is suitable for the occasion. The complete learner is able to 'integrate' the 'dialectical' tension among the four adaptive modes – in this way the experiential learning model becomes a model of *the* complete learner.

I find it difficult to accept this interpretation for two basic reasons. First, it seems to make sense only in a very general, abstract way such as when one is discussing changes in the self and how it adapts to the world. As noted earlier, the experiential learning model does not apply to every concrete learning situation we encounter, that is, not every learning situation demands a balanced integration of concrete experience, reflective observation, abstract conceptualisation and active experimentation. However, most learning situations can be described in terms of one or more of these 'adaptive modes'; thus the experiential learning model is best conceived as a classification scheme than as a model of learning. Second, existing empirical support for the model is weak. The Learning Style Inventory has no capacity to measure the degree of integration of learning styles. Indeed, it really only measures the relative preference of one set of words over another in describing learning styles. It is certainly not a measure of learning style competence; it is a measure of preference only so it is conceivable that person 'A' as a converger will be better at divergent thinking than person 'B' who is a diverger. This limitation of the Learning Style Inventory constrains the extent to which it can be used to support the experiential learning model. Finally, the applicability of the model to different cultures is not apparent. Anderson (1988) for example highlights the need to recognise different culturally based cognitive and communication styles, especially the difference between western and non-western styles as opposed to the typology offered by Kolb and Fry.

These objections do not preclude the possibility of using the experiential learning model to inform adult education practice. As a rule of thumb the model provides an excellent framework for planning teaching and learning activities and it can be usefully employed as a guide for understanding learning difficulties, vocational counselling, academic advising and so on. But one needs to be careful and avoid accepting the model in its entirety because it can lead to a number of misconceptions about learners. For example, that everyone has a learning style which narrows their capacity as a learner, or that some learners are incapable of integrating their knowledge because they are at a lower stage of psychological development; or, finally, that there are two 'classes' of learner, the privileged class (who can integrate their knowledge) and the less privileged class (who are not capable of this integration).

CONCLUDING REMARKS

At the close of the section on field dependence/independence I remarked that learning style information should be shared with the learners. This view is also espoused by Dixon (1985) who argues that we should abandon the 'instructor-controlled' implementation model of learning style information. Nevertheless, she does specify a role for the instructor, whose responsibilities are:

1 Helping individuals understand themselves as learners (e.g. through the critical application of learning style inventories and through introspection).
2 Encouraging individuals to expand their learning styles (e.g. by discussing learning strategies with students).
3 Using a variety of instructional approaches (so that learners experience different ways of learning).
4 Creating an environment in which diversity can thrive (e.g. through the creative use of learning contracts).
5 Creating a climate in which collaboration exists (e.g. by using others as resources).

These principles remain, in my view, the best statement to date on how best to apply learning style information to adult education practices.

Chapter 7

Behaviourism

Gauging the initial reaction of people to different psychological theories can be very instructive. For example, psychoanalysis is often peremptorily dismissed as an affront to common-sense knowledge, a reaction which is typically diluted with further exploration. By way of contrast, the vocabulary of behaviourism (conditioning, reward, punishment, stimulus, response) is usually received sympathetically because it is consistent with the casual observations we make about human behaviour. It is only when the origin of this vocabulary is made explicit that we balk and reassess our position. This chapter is the product of just such a reassessment.

It is usual to attribute the beginning of behaviourism to John Watson, who published 'Psychology as the behaviourist views it' in 1913. He argued, as did others to follow, that psychology should be redefined as the study of behaviour and that it should abandon the examination of inaccessible and unobservable mental events. In this way the scientific obligation to be 'objective' would be fulfilled. Watson assumed that most of our behaviour is acquired through learning, which is to say that it is the result of environmental rather than biological influences. Thus the study of learning and the conditions under which it occurs became the core project of behaviourism. Naturally, the type of learning which attracted the attention of the behaviourists was the acquisition of stereotyped responses (e.g. Pavlov's dogs salivating when a bell rings) and the acquisition of observable and quantifiable skills and knowledge (e.g. recalling a list of nonsense syllables). Also, in order to identify the environmental influences on learning it was necessary to conduct experiments in carefully controlled environments. The logic of this approach ruled out investigating humans in a natural setting, the law (or professional ethics) rules out investigating humans in the laboratory setting and so the natural candidate for learning experiments was the laboratory animal, usually the albino cat, dog, pigeon or rhesus monkey.

Using animals in a laboratory setting to discover the principles of learning is a hallmark of the behaviourist method. The most widely known 'classic' experiments are those of the Russian physiologist Pavlov (1927), who 'conditioned' a dog to salivate to the sound of a bell, and the American psychologist Skinner (1938), who enticed rats and pigeons to press or peck a lever to obtain pellets of feed in an apparatus which is now known as the 'Skinner Box'. For the present purpose, Skinner's work will be taken as representing the behaviourist paradigm. This is because, first, he embodies the most extreme or radical form of behaviourism and, second, his views have had a direct impact on educational theory and teaching practice.

Skinner argues that organisms simply emit responses which are gradually shaped by their consequences. When a response (bit of behaviour) has a rewarding (reinforcing) consequence, it is more likely to occur again; when it has a non-rewarding consequence, it is less likely to occur again. In this way we acquire a repertoire of behaviour which is literally 'shaped' by the environment. This process is best exemplified by considering Skinner's early experiments with animals.

A typical experiment is to place a hungry pigeon in an isolated and sound-proof box containing a rather prominent button which, if pecked, will result in a food pellet being dispensed into a tray. The pigeon is allowed to wander about unhindered, pecking here and there as pigeons do. In these circumstances the pigeon will eventually peck at the button and receive a food pellet. With each successful peck at the button, the pigeon will be more likely to abandon its random pecking behaviour and stand before the food tray, alternately pecking at the button and eating the grain. Skinner, in effect, makes a reinforcing consequence (the food pellet) contingent upon a certain behaviour (pecking the button) and observes the result. In this experimental setting he has complete control over the consequences of the pigeon's behaviour; in his terminology, he is able to vary the contingencies of reinforcement and observe the resulting behaviour. By doing just this, Skinner is able to plot the relationships between behaviour and reinforcement, and to develop a vocabulary expressing these relationships. Some examples are as follows:

1 If the apparatus is readjusted so that no food pellet is delivered after the button is pecked, the pigeon will cease pecking at the button (i.e. extinction will occur).
2 If the button is illuminated each time a pellet of food is delivered, then the pigeon will peck at the button when it illuminates only, and ceases to deliver a pellet of food. In this instance the illumination itself becomes reinforcing and is called a *secondary reinforcer* to distinguish it from the *primary reinforcer* (food pellet) which was responsible for the original learning.
3 If we manually control the food dispenser, we can deliver a pellet of food every time the pigeon approaches the button. By making the reinforcement contingent on successively closer approaches to the button we can 'channel' or 'shape' the pigeon's behaviour towards the desired response of pecking the button. This is called *shaping*.

4 The pattern of reinforcement can be varied and its effects on learning and extinction observed. The pattern of reinforcement can vary along a continuum from 100 per cent (every peck of the button is reinforced) to zero (no pecks of the button are reinforced). For example, the mechanism may be set to reinforce every tenth peck, or some time interval may be required (say, a minute) before a peck will activate the food dispenser. In addition, the number of pecks required to activate the food dispenser may be varied from trial to trial or even randomised so that no regular pattern is discernible. The time interval can be similarly varied. These are all instances of *partial reinforcement*. If partial reinforcement is used, learning occurs more slowly but it persists for longer after reinforcement is discontinued. In the extreme case, where reinforcement occurs randomly, the response continues indefinitely, at least until the experimenter rescues the pigeon from its plight by removing it from the box altogether.

In scenarios like the above, Skinner is intent on uncovering the empirical relationship between reinforcement and behaviour; as such, his approach is atheoretical, and for him the study of learning ends when one has identified the various types of conditioning and the principles by which they operate.

The criticism Skinner attracts is mainly due to his application of the technical vocabulary of the laboratory to the broad sweep of human behaviour. He claims that we should dispense with vague 'mentalistic' terms such as wants, needs, wishes, ideas, will, purpose and intention and reinterpret them in the language of reinforcement and its contingencies. In the most readable account of the significance of his work, *Beyond Freedom and Dignity*, Skinner (1973) supplies us with a sample of what he has in mind. Here he is describing a person who is experiencing a host of difficulties:

> he lacks assurance or feels insecure or is unsure of himself (his behaviour is weak and inappropriate); he is dissatisfied or discouraged (he is seldom reinforced and as a result his behaviour undergoes extinction); he is frustrated (extinction is accompanied by emotional responses); he feels uneasy or anxious (his behaviour frequently has unavoidable aversive consequences which have emotional effects); there is nothing he wants to do or enjoys doing well, he has no feeling of craftsmanship, no sense of leading a purposeful life, no sense of accomplishment (he is rarely reinforced for doing anything); he feels guilty or ashamed (he has previously been punished for idleness or failure, which now evokes emotional responses): he is disappointed in himself or disgusted with himself (he is no longer reinforced by the admiration of others, and the extinction which follows has emotional effects).

(Skinner 1973: 144)

In a later section of the same publication he asserts that the notion of a 'self' as the originator of action is misguided and that 'identity' is reducible to a

> repertoire of behaviour appropriate to a given set of contingencies. The picture which emerges from a scientific analysis is not of a body with a person inside, but of a body which is a person in the sense that it displays a complex repertoire of behaviour.
>
> (Skinner 1973: 194–5)

Thus, for Skinner, the scope of his work is unlimited and there is nothing in the human condition which can escape his analysis. If he were less articulate or influential he may well have been ignored; as it is, his views have provoked vehement criticism. The two most important lines of criticism focus on the shortcomings of his experimental paradigm and the limited explanatory power of his technical vocabulary.

DEFICITS IN THE EXPERIMENTAL PARADIGM

Braginsky and Braginsky (1974) outline two related objections to the type of laboratory experiment utilised by Skinner:

> In this environment, behaviour is not examined from the point of view of the organism who is behaving (i.e. how it feels about what it is doing, or how it interprets its own behaviour) or from the social context in which the organism is interacting (i.e. the social forces that are present in the interaction between the researcher and his subject).
>
> (Braginsky and Braginsky 1974: 46–7)

For practical reasons alone these considerations must be dismissed when experimenting with animals. However, the heart of the matter is that Skinner feels justified in making generalisations about human beings on the basis of results obtained in the experimental laboratory. The objection to this is not that humans are different from animals, but that the artificial and tightly controlled laboratory environment is different from everyday life. An important aspect of everyday life is that interactions occur between people, and to make sense of these we need to know something about the social context in which they occur and the perceptions of the parties concerned.

Even Skinner, unwittingly, makes assumptions about the context of his laboratory experiments. On the face of it there is nothing in the Skinnerian logic which would prevent us from reinterpreting his observations in a perverse way (as cartoonists have done); and construe the experimenter's behaviour as being 'conditioned' by the pigeon pecking the disc.

But we do not do this because we perceive the experimenter to be the agent who dispenses reinforcement and controls the proceedings.

Skinner's animals are always placed in a position where the consequences of their actions appear to be the result of the 'way things are' and not caused by another organism, such as the experimenter. But when an animal or human perceives an agent or person to be the cause of their pain or pleasure, then their behaviour changes quite dramatically, as Martin (1980) observes:

> If you arrange a mechanical dispenser of dog biscuits which your puppy then learns to operate, it is justifiable to claim that he is instrumentally conditioned. If, however, you invariably dispense his biscuits by hand so that you appear in the event as an agent, he will come to fawn on you in a way quite different from the way he treats the food dispenser. There is, then, a distinction to be made between conditioning in its technical sense and reward and punishment, because in the latter case the responsibility as a person or agent for the pain or pleasure enters the perception of the organism being manipulated.
>
> (Martin 1980: 113)

Skinner is careful to avoid such loose terms as 'reward' and 'punishment' because they imply all manner of mentalistic notions having to do with agents and the perception of agency. But Martin argues, quite correctly, that the term 'reinforcement' should be restricted in its use to describing those instances where there is no perceived agent dispensing pellets of food or whatever. It may be appropriate for the Skinner Box, but it has little generalisability beyond that context.

EXPLANATORY POWER

There are three general considerations which lead us to question the explanatory power of a Skinnerian approach. First, there are a range of phenomena which appear to resist a conditioning explanation. For example, there are those instances where skills are used in a highly flexible way, as in the use of language; there are those cases where people do things which lead only to intangible rewards; and there are all those cases where people appear to learn passively, by observing others' actions rather than responding to the consequences of their own actions. Dissatisfaction with Skinner's explanation for each of these, but particularly the last mentioned, resulted in a considerable reworking of his approach among learning theorists. For example, Bandura (1969) found it necessary to acknowledge the importance of internal cognitive variables to explain observational learning. Observational learning is learning which occurs through observing the consequences of others' behaviour. Typically the observers gain an inkling of the pattern of rewards and punishments which will come their way should they imitate another's behaviour. This brings us to the second general consideration concerning the explanatory power of behaviourism

– whether alternative explanations can be offered for the various 'conditioning' experiments.

Martin, for one, has constructed an alternative explanation for the different degrees of resistance to extinction associated with different patterns of reinforcement. He regards the organism as a pattern perceiver:

> The most easily discerned pattern of events is that in which reinforcement follows every peck at the button (100% reinforcement). The peck and the delivery of grain appear as two events which are invariably linked in time. If we then shut off reinforcement completely each subsequent peck at the button can be regarded as an experiment (on the bird's part) which has negative results. Under these conditions, extinction is rapid, and we should suggest that this is because each peck produces a lot of information about the new state of the environment. In extinction trials which follow learning under, say, 25% reinforced trials, four pecks could be necessary to acquire the same amount of information.
>
> (Martin 1980: 114)

This reasoning can be applied to explain the effects on extinction of all the possible combinations of partial reinforcement. It is an explanation which is unacceptable to Skinner because it presupposes that the organism guides its own behaviour according to the patterns it discovers in the world. And yet it is a plausible presupposition, especially given some of the aspects of human behaviour cited earlier, such as the capacity of humans to learn through observing others – which may lead them to refrain from unacceptable behaviour without experiencing punishment or strive to gain a reward never previously experienced. One could multiply examples like these, but the general point is already made that the behaviour of animals in a 'Skinner Box' can be explained without recourse to the term 'conditioning' and that this is also true of human behaviour in a natural setting.

A third consideration in evaluating the explanatory power of behaviourism is the status of its technical vocabulary. It was noted earlier that Skinner advocates translating the vocabulary of everyday life into the vocabulary of behaviourism. The discourse of behaviourism appears to be sterile and mechanistic, but it would be tolerable if it aided our understanding. But does it? A useful approach in answering this question is to consider more closely a basic concept, reinforcement, and how it is used in the principle referred to as the 'law of conditioning', which in a paraphrased form reads: 'if the occurrence of a bit of behaviour is followed by the presence of a reinforcing stimulus, the strength of that behaviour is increased' (Skinner 1938: 21).

But elsewhere in the same publication Skinner *defines* a reinforcing stimulus by its power to produce this change in response strength. This definition makes the so-called 'law' a tautology. Chomsky makes this assessment:

> The phrase 'X is reinforced by Y (stimulus, state of affairs, event, etc.)' is being used as a cover term for 'X wants Y', 'X likes Y', 'X wishes that Y were the case', etc. Invoking the term 'reinforcement' has no explanatory force, and any idea that this paraphrase introduces any new clarity or objectivity into the description of wishing, liking, etc. is a serious delusion.
>
> (Chomsky 1959: 38)

Other terms in the behaviourist vernacular such as 'stimulus', 'response' and 'conditioning' have been subjected to the same type of criticism, but in spite of this 'conditioning' is still frequently invoked to explain human behaviour, and it is particularly favoured among educationalists and others with an interest in behavioural control. In adult education its influence is most apparent in the literature on behavioural objectives, which is the subject of the remainder of this chapter.

BEHAVIOURAL OBJECTIVES

There is something very compelling in the proposition that, at the commencement of learning, both the teacher and learner should be clear about the intent. A clear intent implies a goal or objective which can be used for developing learning activities and measuring progress and achievement. Moreover, keeping the learner informed (or, better still, involved in setting objectives) is surely an open, honest and democratic thing to do. By contrast, an authoritarian approach obscures the intent of learning. Teachers are free to shift the ground-rules according to their every whim and learners are rendered impotent as they become enmeshed in an elaborate guessing game about 'what the teacher really wants us to learn'. Given the above, it seems odd that some commentators have rejected learning objectives as being incompatible with the best traditions of adult education (Huberman 1974; MacDonald-Ross 1975; Robinson and Taylor 1983). When this rejection is apparent, it is normally voiced about a particular type of learning objective, the 'behavioural objective'.

The vocabulary of behavioural objectives sits very comfortably with the behaviourist tradition, and it serves a similar function. This is illustrated by the following passage from Gronlund:

> Let's try another pair of statements to be sure you can tell the difference between behavioural and non-behavioural terms. Which one of the following clearly indicates a behavioural statement?
>
> 1 Predicts the outcome of an experiment.
> 2 Sees the value of an experiment.

This time you should have had little difficulty in selecting the first statement as the correct answer. The term 'sees' is a common one in education (e.g. 'I see the point'), and its familiarity might have misled you. But note that 'sees' refers to an internal state. What observable behaviour will the student exhibit when he 'sees' the value of an experiment? Will he describe its usefulness, point out its theoretical implications, or estimate the social consequences of the results? We simply can't tell because the term 'sees' is vague, indefinite, and describes a reaction that is not directly observable.

(Gronlund 1985: 13)

Like the behaviourist there is an emphasis on removing from the vocabulary terms which refer to internal states. The reason is that such terms are not directly observable and therefore it is impossible to tell whether learning objectives are being achieved. The argument is that learning outcomes can best be described in terms of changes in the learner's behaviour. What is needed, then, is a set of guidelines for teachers and learners to help them state their learning intent unambiguously. The way to do this is to formulate objectives using verbs that refer to observable behaviour only. We cannot observe someone 'recognising' or 'knowing' something, but we can observe them 'identifying' or 'describing' something – so the latter terms are preferred. It is permissible to use such vague terms as 'applies', 'comprehends', 'knows' and 'understands', but only if they are further defined by a list of the types of behaviour students are to demonstrate when the objectives have been achieved. Thus:

There are several things to remember about *specific learning outcomes.* . . . First is that, like the general objective, each statement begins with a verb. Here, however, the verbs are specific and indicate definite observable responses; that is, responses that can be seen and evaluated by an outside observer. These verbs are listed here to show what is meant by stating the specific learning outcomes in terms of observable pupil performance.

- Describes
- Identifies
- States
- Distinguishes
- Explains

Terms such as these clarify what the pupils will do to demonstrate their *understanding*. Such vague terms such as *realizes, sees,* and *believes* are less useful in defining objectives because they describe internal states that can be expressed by many different types of overt behaviour.

(Gronlund and Linn 1990: 37)

Another point of contact with behaviourism is that behavioural objectives are seen to be appropriate for every conceivable type of learning. An instance of this is when Gronlund supplies us with an exhaustive list of illustrative verbs for stating specific learning outcomes for 'creative behaviours', 'drama behaviours', 'music behaviours', 'complex, logical, judgmental behaviours', 'social behaviours' and many others. Another instance can be found in Bloom's (1956) well-known *Taxonomy of Educational Objectives*, which, in its successive revisions over the years, represents an attempt to categorise all possible learning outcomes in a matrix of 'domains' and 'levels' of knowledge. It is this rather ambitious claim for the role of behavioural objectives (a claim which is echoed in training programmes for adult educators) which prompts critical comment.

A reservation commonly expressed about behavioural objectives is that they fragment learning into narrowly conceived categories of behaviour which lose 'sight of the forest of skilled competence for the trees of perfected performances' (Bruner 1971: 113). The distinction between competence and performance is important here. Even staunch advocates of behavioural objectives insist that the learning outcomes being measured should reflect the underlying competence of the learner (in this respect they differ from their behaviourist counterparts). But do behavioural objectives offer us the best method for measuring competence? There are several reasons for believing that they do not.

The first reason is that all the behavioural indicators of competence can rarely be determined in advance. People express their competence, in whatever field, in a variety of imaginative and unpredictable ways. Conversely they can be blocked from demonstrating their competence for apparently trivial reasons. For example, if we wish to measure the logical reasoning competence of a learner, we may specify a behavioural objective such as: 'To identify the validity or invalidity of a set of "conclusions" derived from a corresponding set of premises (without error and under test conditions).' And we may require the learner to identify the validity of the following argument:

> If God exists, then he is everywhere.
> God is not everywhere.
> Therefore God does not exist.

Religious people have difficulty correctly identifying the validity of the above conclusion – not because they are incompetent at reasoning logically, but because they have a strong belief in the falsity of the conclusion. They generally perform better on syllogisms without a religious content (Feather 1964). There are two points which can be drawn from this example. First, we cannot generalise from 'behaviour' to 'competence' without taking into account the context in which the behaviour occurs, and it is impossible to control or predict every aspect of the context (e.g. learner's motivation, past experience, variables associated with the testing situation). Second, because the context is largely unpredictable, we should not limit ourselves to pre-planned conceptions of what is, and what is not, a fair behavioural indicator of competence.

The second reason is that the emphasis on terminal learning outcomes undervalues the importance of the learning process. The preoccupation with the end point of instruction is mitigated somewhat by what are called 'enabling' objectives, which refer to assessable marker points along the learning path. The difficulty with this is that people learn at different rates and have different styles of learning, so any predetermined, uniform monitoring of progress is likely to favour some and hinder others. It is not simply that these tests are unfair, but that, because of their focus on observable behaviour, they do an injustice to the complexity of learning. For example, in mastering a complex skill, such as playing the piano, learning can proceed along a multitude of dimensions – posture, finger position, notation, use of the pedal, scale drill, chord progressions, and so on. However, not all these dimensions can be separated for instructional purposes; even if this were the case it would be wrong to measure progress along each separate dimension as an indicator of progress towards the ultimate objective. This is because what is most important in learning complex skills is how the various dimensions 'come together' to form an integrated whole. And it is precisely this type of outcome which resists behavioural analysis. It becomes necessary to employ so called 'imprecise' and 'vague' terms to assist learning and measure progress.

The third reason is that not all learning outcomes are specifiable in behavioural terms. Bruner (1966), in his classic essay on *The Process of Education*, outlines two ways in which learning can serve us in the future.

One is through its specific applicability to tasks that are highly similar to those we originally learned to perform. Psychologists refer to this phenomenon as *specific transfer* of training; perhaps it should be called the extension of habits or associations. Its utility appears to be limited in the main to what we usually speak of as skills. Having learned how to hammer nails, we are better able later to learn how to hammer tacks or chip wood. Learning in school undoubtedly creates skills of a kind that transfer to activities encountered later, either in school or after. A second way in which earlier learning renders later performance more efficient is through what is conveniently called *non-specific transfer*, or, more accurately, the transfer of principles and attitudes. In essence, it consists of learning initially not a skill but a general idea, which can then be used as a basis for recognizing subsequent problems as special cases of the idea originally mastered.

(Bruner 1966: 17)

Behavioural objectives, because they relate only to the specific observable outcomes of learning, cannot address adequately the acquisition of the basic and general ideas referred to above.

This is because these ideas can have meaning only in terms of a general and abstract level of discourse. For example, a valued learning outcome among industrial trainers is 'safety consciousness'. But what is meant by this? Can we reduce it to a specific set of performance indicators such as 'describes the procedure to be followed in an emergency' or 'lists the safety rules of the workshop'? I doubt it – no matter how exhaustive and valuable our list of performance indicators, they can never collectively capture the spirit of 'safety consciousness'. We must make recourse to terms like 'values', 'appreciates', 'feels', or 'understands' in order to give expression to what we mean by 'safety consciousness'. True, we can assess it only by observing people's behaviour, but we cannot specify what this behaviour will be – beyond describing, in abstract terms, the principles to which the behaviour must conform.

Another line of argument is that objectives, almost by definition, cannot be derived for subjective outcomes like 'development of self-concept' (Robinson and Taylor 1983). What are the performance indicators of an improved self-concept? Our judgements about such things are derived from a complex array of observations, their connections and the inferences we make from them. We could attempt to operationalise the concept but this would require us to select a few key performance indicators from an infinite variety of possible observations. Such an exercise would be artificial and futile, and it would do an injustice to the complexity of what we mean by 'self-concept'.

The fourth reason is that learning may be occurring which is not being measured. In many respects behavioural objectives constrain our assessment of the benefits of any learning effort. The implication is that if we fail to achieve our objectives, the learning effort is wasted. Or, alternatively, that the objectives we achieve are the most important outcomes of the learning effort. Neither of these statements acknowledges the importance of unplanned or incidental learning. No teacher, or learner for that matter, has complete control over what is being learnt. Valuable learning can, and often does, occur which is outside the original intent. This type of learning should be acknowledged when evaluating any learning experience – but it is typically overlooked when behavioural objectives are used as a benchmark for success.

Robinson and Taylor (1983) draw attention to the way in which behavioural objectives imply a rational planning model of learning. This model is well exemplified by Davis *et al.* (1974), who describe the steps in designing any learning system (see Table 7.1).

According to the above, learning can, and should, proceed in a logical and orderly manner. Robinson and Taylor (1983) argue that this type of

Table 7.1 The learning system design process

1	Describe current system
2	Derive and write objectives
3	Describe tasks
4	Analyse tasks and objectives
5	Plan evaluation
6	Design instruction
7	Implement instruction
8	Conduct evaluation

Source: adapted from Davis *et al.* (1974: 19)

approach is incompatible with the ethos of adult education for a number of reasons:

1 No account is taken of the unpredictability of student-centred learning, which is characterised by a constant re-definition of goals while exploring learning possibilities.
2 When learners are required to derive their own objectives there is an assumption that they know precisely what and how they want to learn, and that they can articulate their intent.
3 When objectives are specified for the learner they serve as an instrument of institutional control and they support dependency among learners.
4 Objectives function as an authoritarian support for the teacher in the sense that they are part of a controlled learning process where failure can only be the result of the learner's failings.
5 A behavioural objective is an educational tool which helps legitimise the professional nature of adult education. It is closely associated with the culture of accountability, payment by results, cost effectiveness and the 'guaranteed product' of student performance.

The above points certainly establish that behavioural objectives, as a component of the rational model of learning, have a case to answer. The rational model does indeed appear to be opposed to a 'participatory', 'democratic' and 'liberatory' adult education. But it should be said that Robinson and Taylor's comments are directed at a consistently rigorous application of the behavioural objectives approach. The same can be said of the preceding comments in this section. Robinson and Taylor deny the possibility that practitioners can use objectives as guides only – and that they can be modified, challenged, reworked or even abandoned in the pursuit of learning. 'You cannot have a "more or less" model; its credibility depends on an internal consistency, on an internal logic. Put simply, the programme is an objective model or it isn't' (Robinson and Taylor 1983: 358). Ironically, this is the type of rigid demand they profess to criticise in the rational model of learning. By allowing no scope for a flexible and tentative application of objectives, the critics seal their case. This is a legitimate thing to do, but there is always the danger of assuming that what is 'logically' necessary, is necessary in practice. In practice, behavioural objectives applied in a certain way *may* be entirely consistent with what we judge to be good adult education practice. The foregoing arguments simply indicate the improbability of this occurring, especially when practice rigidly follows the guidelines in the literature currently available.

Similar arguments have been advanced in relation to the nature of competency-based education. Many eminent educationalists (e.g. Collins 1991; Eraut 1993; Newman 1994) have attacked the competency movement as being too technicist, mechanistic, reductionist and atheoretical. These arguments have force if a certain view of competence is adopted – that it consists of the capacity to undertake certain well-defined tasks associated with a particular occupation. However, others have argued (Gonczi *et al.* 1993; Gonczi 1994; Hager and Beckett 1995) that competence need not be defined in such a narrow way. It is possible to view competence in a more integrated and holistic way whereby it comprises the application in particular contexts of individuals' underlying attributes (knowledge, skills attitudes and values). As such, competence is conceived of as relational: it brings together individual attributes and the contexts in which these attributes are realised. Individuals are deemed competent if they can bring together complex combinations of their knowledge, values, attitudes and skills in a way appropriate to the contexts in which they are required to act. A competency-based curriculum, then, in contrast to a behaviourist curriculum, does not specify a range of competencies or tasks to be mastered. Instead, a set of competency standards is developed which forms the backdrop to the curriculum. It can also be argued that the notion of competence brings together theory and practice, and that it acknowledges the important role of workplace learning and learning from experience more broadly. Thus it allows scope for the recognition of prior learning and the articulation of learning gained from work and nonformal education into the formal sector. I am mentioning this, not to support the competency-based movement, but to highlight the danger of rejecting, without serious engagement with the arguments, either behavioural objectives or competency-based education as necessarily antithetical to the broader values of adult education.

Chapter 8

Group dynamics and the group facilitator

Group dynamics, as a field of inquiry within social psychology, is said to occupy the 'middle ground' between the person and society. This is because it is the small group which becomes the unit of analysis, the crucible, so to speak, which reveals the secrets of how the person forms, and is formed by, the social environment. A basic premise in group dynamics is that a group is more than a mere collection of individuals, that is, groups have their own dynamic quite independent of the individuals comprising them. Many theoretical perspectives and research techniques have been applied to the study of groups. It comes as no surprise to find that the various approaches to understanding group phenomena and the explanations advanced are as diverse within the field of group dynamics as they are in psychology generally. However, I wish to avoid a lengthy exposition of these different perspectives which would, in any case, require a repetition of much of what has already been said. For this reason the approach adopted in this chapter will be to explore the significance of groups for adult educators, and the way in which group dynamic concepts have been (or could be) used as a foundation for practice.

THE INDIVIDUAL AND THE GROUP IN ADULT EDUCATION

In contemporary adult education there is a tension between the ethic of individualism and the spirit of collectivism. Individualism is most apparent in the humanistic approach. This was touched upon earlier but is worth expanding here. The core ideas of the ethic of individualism are described by Lukes (1973). First, there 'is the ultimate moral principle of the supreme and intrinsic value, or dignity of the individual human being' (Lukes 1973: 45). This constitutes a moral axiom which places the individual at the centre of a value system which relegates the 'group' to second place. Second, there is 'the notion of autonomy, or self-direction, according to which an individual's thought and action is his own, and not determined by agencies or causes outside his control' (1973: 51). And finally, there is the notion of self-development which is steeped in the romantic tradition and which

> specified an ideal for the lives of individuals – an ideal whose content varies with different ideas of the self on a continuum from pure egoism to strong communitarianism. It is either anti-social, with the individual set apart from and hostile to society, or extra-social, when the individual pursues his own path, free of social pressures; or highly social, where the individual's self-development is achieved through community with others.
>
> (Lukes 1973: 71)

These three features of individualism – the dignity of the person, autonomy and self-direction, and self-development – underlie the value system implicit in humanistic adult education. Ironically, this value system is widespread among adult educators who nevertheless profess an understanding of groups and a commitment to group work. Symptomatic of this 'individualist' approach to groups is a conception of group work as a means to an end. The claim is that group learning is better than, say, the lecture format, because it encourages the pooling of resources, builds a sense of group belonging, allows participants to express their views, helps them to clarify their thinking, and so on. The adult educator's task is to develop an armoury of group teaching techniques, a sensitivity to the pitfalls of group work, and an ability to intervene appropriately in the group process. The ultimate aim is to establish a smoothly functioning, cohesive group in which individuals can work together and learn productively. The group dynamics literature offers an abundance of supportive material on conformity, group cohesion, leadership, communication structures, the emergence of norms, group development, group decision making, and individual versus group performance – all of which can be used in the service of understanding how the individual is influenced by the group or how a particular individual (the facilitator) can influence the life of the group.

The collectivist spirit is best exemplified in the writings of 'radical' adult educators such as Freire (1972), Gelpi (1979), Lovett et al. (1983) and Griffin (1987). They are interested in how adult education can contribute to radical social change and how it can foster collective, as opposed to individual, advancement. Historical precedents often cited as models of collective adult education are the Highlander Folk School in Tennessee, the Antigonish movement in Nova Scotia, the Labour Colleges in the USA, the Scandinavian Study Circles and the Danish co-operatives. The collectivist's spirit is overtly political in the sense that it advocates the empowerment of certain groups in society, such as the working class, peasants, women; and racial, indigenous or religious minorities. It is also opposed to adult education initiatives which are solely used as vehicles for personal advancement, which, in the final analysis, will produce only 'clever rogues'. This commitment to the group originates from a political ideology which emphasises the importance of democratic leadership, participation in decision making, co-operative activities and self-management. The foundations for practice here are political and social theory, rather than social psychology or group dynamics. The idea of group self-determination is a political and moral imperative and the purpose of group work is not so much to promote group cohesion or arrive at some kind of consensus, as to provide a forum for democratic discussion and decision making.

These two approaches to the group, the 'individualistic' and the 'collective', are best conceived as opposite ends of a continuum along which real life adult educators may be positioned. The literature on group dynamics is, on balance, more easily identified with the 'individualistic' pole of this continuum. It corresponds to what Olmsted and Hare (1978) refer to as the 'internal' approach to groups:

> The second approach to the study of groups may be referred to as the 'internal' focus on groups as societies. This is a newer, experimentally minded tradition and derives from psychology more than from sociology. Groups are conceived of as worth studying because they are relevant environments for individual behaviour – they are the sub societies in which social interaction and the individual's part in it can be observed and tested.

> (Olmsted and Hare 1978: 9)

This 'internal' approach to the group (as opposed to the 'external' approach, which is concerned with how groups function in larger social entities) has yielded a mass of research data and a diverse range of theoretical explanations. There now exist a number of standard 'classic' texts which provide a relatively coherent picture of the field (e.g. Cartwright and Zander 1968; Hare 1976; Shaw 1981) and there are some texts specifically relating group dynamics to adult learning (e.g. McLeish et al. 1973; Cooper 1975; Jaques 1992).

The interest of adult educators in group dynamics stems from a belief that it is through group learning that many of the precepts in adult education can be realised. Groups are said to promote self-understanding through shared support and mutual feedback. They generate the experiential base for learning; they encourage interaction, self-determination and trust. It is the group that challenges the traditional relationship between the teacher and the taught and insists on equal input into planning. Ultimately, it is only through the group that 'learning how to learn' can be achieved. Given these beliefs, the primacy given to group dynamics in the training of adult educators is understandable, even though only a brief acquaintance with the literature will reveal that each of these beliefs can be challenged.

Adult learning texts, when they refer to group dynamics, tend to select material which will assist the adult educator to

1 Observe groups (e.g. Bales' Interaction Process Analysis, Moreno's Sociometry technique).
2 Interpret their observations (e.g. as a phase of group development, an instance of group influence, an indication of role differentiation, etc.).
3 Intervene in the group process (e.g. Heron's Six Category Intervention Analysis, the myriad of group teaching techniques, the Nominal Group Technique).

The remainder of this chapter will focus on the last of the above purposes and consider some common group facilitation techniques and the more general questions they raise.

GROUP INFLUENCE AND EXPERIENTIAL TECHNIQUES

There is a tradition of research in group dynamics which documents the powerful influence of the group on individual actions, perceptions, judgements and beliefs. There are some landmark studies in this literature and it is worth reviewing a sample of them briefly prior to discussing the nature of the experiential group.

The classic experiment in this tradition was conducted by Sherif (1935). Subjects are seated in a darkened room and required to track the apparent movement of a spot of light. The light is in fact stationary and its apparent movement is an optical illusion known as the autokinetic effect (a small stationary spot of light in a dark room normally appears to move between 50 mm and 150 mm). When alone, individuals gradually establish a range (say 75–125 mm) and a norm (say, 100 mm) for their judgements. When people who have established such ranges and norms are brought together in groups, their ranges and norms converge into a group norm. It is the group norm which persists when subjects are asked once again to judge individually. The significance of this experiment is that it is the group norm which has a more binding force than individual norms.

A later but equally celebrated set of studies is reported by Asch (1956). In his experiments subjects are asked to judge which of three vertical lines (of 15.5 cm, 20 cm and 17 cm) is equivalent in length to a standard vertical line of 20 cm. Subjects can perform this task with 100 per cent accuracy when judging alone. However, when the judgement occurs in a group where the other members unanimously give an incorrect judgement (because they are confederates of the experimenter), approximately one-third of the subjects go against their own senses and conform to the majority judgement for at least half the trials. This level of conformity is strikingly reduced when the subject has an 'ally' who disagrees with the majority judgement and insists on judging correctly. No satisfactory explanation for the level of yielding has been advanced to date. At the time Asch (1956) suggested that three types of yielding were apparent:

1 Those whose perceptions were actually distorted and therefore perceived the majority estimates as correct.
2 Those who accepted the correctness of the group judgement but realised that they perceived something different.
3 Those who believed their judgement to be correct but went along with the majority decision to avoid appearing different.

These distinctions correspond to attempts made elsewhere to classify processes of group influence such as internalisation, where the individual takes on the values of the group; identification, where the individual desires to be like the group; and compliance, where the individual 'obeys' the group norms to avoid rejection (Douglas 1989). Despite the limitations of these earlier studies (e.g. that the groups being studied were really not 'groups' in the proper sense) they nevertheless remain powerful demonstrations of group influence.

Deception is a key research technique for many of the studies on group influence. One researcher who employed deception to an extreme (and some say unethical) degree was Milgram (1965). He was interested in the conditions under which people would or would not carry out another's command. The essential elements of the study are described by Milgram:

The focus of the study concerns the amount of electric shock a subject is willing to administer to another person when ordered by an experimenter to give the 'victim' increasingly more severe punishment. The act of administering shock is set in the context of a learning experiment, ostensibly designed to study the effect of punishment on memory. Aside from the experimenter, one naive subject and one accomplice perform in each session. On arrival each subject is paid $4.50. After a general talk by the experimenter, telling how little scientists know about the effect of punishment on memory, subjects are informed that one member of the pair will serve as teacher and one as a learner. A rigged drawing is held so that the naive subject is always the teacher, and the accomplice becomes the learner. The learner is taken to an adjacent room and strapped into an 'electric chair'.

The naive subject is told that it is his task to teach the learner a list of paired associates, to test him on the list, and to administer punishment whenever the learner errs in the test. Punishment takes the form of electric shock, delivered to the learner by means of a shock generator controlled by the naive subject. The teacher is instructed to increase the intensity of electric shock one step on the generator on each error. The learner, according to plan, provides many wrong answers, so that before long the naive subject must give him the strongest shock on the generator. Increases in shock level are met by increasingly insistent demands from the learner that the experiment be stopped because of the growing discomfort to him (the deception is that the 'learner' in fact receives no shocks at all). The responses of the victim are standardised on tape, and each protest is co-ordinated to a particular voltage level on the shock generator. Starting with 75 volts the learner begins to grunt and moan. At 150 volts he demands to be let out of the experiment. At 180 volts he cries out that he can no longer stand the pain. At 300 volts he refuses to provide any more answers to the memory test, insisting that he is no longer a participant in the experiment and must be freed. In response to his last tactic, the experimenter instructs the naive subject to treat the absence of an answer as equivalent to a wrong answer, and to follow the usual shock procedure The experimenter reinforces his demand with the statement: 'You have no other choice, you must go on!' (This imperative is used whenever the naive subject tries to break off the experiment.) If the subject refuses to give the next higher level of shock, the experiment is considered at an end.

(Milgram 1965: 59–60)

Using this procedure Milgram reports that over 60 per cent of subjects continue to administer the shocks obediently (although with considerable discomfort and some degree of protest), until instructed to stop by the experimenter. The most striking feature of this experiment (apart from Milgram's apparent disregard for the suffering of the naive subjects) is the high proportion of people willing to carry out the experimenter's instructions, even though they believe their actions are causing considerable pain to another person. Variations on the basic design of the experiment reveal that obedience decreases as the physical proximity of the learner (who is receiving the shocks) increases and as the physical proximity of the experimenter (who is giving the orders to continue) decreases. From the point of view of group influence, the most significant variation on the basic design involves the use of groups. When Milgram arranged for a group of disobedient cohorts to defy the experimenter's authority in the presence of the subjects, then 90 per cent of the subjects followed suit and also defied the experimenter (a group of obedient cohorts increased the subjects' obedience only slightly).

Another experiment looked at the effect of group decisions about an agreed course of action on the subsequent actions of its members. During the Second World War the US government wished to change the eating habits of its population towards the consumption of poultry and meat offal. Lewin (1958), arguing that norms emerge at a group level, suggested trying to change eating habits through group discussion. He then sought to demonstrate the effectiveness of group discussion by comparing it with the effects obtained through using lectures. One group of subjects (all subjects were described as Red Cross volunteer housewives) were treated to a well-prepared lecture on the desirability of diet change and how to prepare recipes which were attractive. A second group of subjects were allowed to discuss the relevance of domestic diet to the war effort, they exchanged ideas and opinions about offal and took a vote on whether they would experiment with a new diet. Interviews carried out a week later show clearly the effectiveness of group discussions: 32 per cent of the group discussion members had actually served one of the recommended meals, which compares with only 3 per cent of the subjects who received a lecture on the subject.

From each of the four experiments mentioned above, one can trace a line of research activity and debate which is still in progress. Like so many social psychological experiments, they function very much like parables. They are now enshrined in the history of social psychology, and are used as a reminder of how individual choice and independent action are shaped and constrained by groups.

Thus we return to an earlier theme relating to whose interests are served by working and learning in groups. Group facilitators in adult education often refer to the desirability of group cohesiveness, which normally means the extent to which group members are attracted to the group. The positive consequences of group cohesiveness are well documented for experimental, learning and working groups and group cohesion is often portrayed as an important step in the growth of groups towards maturity. Given this, it is understandable that group exercises have emerged which have as their primary goal the enhancement of group cohesiveness. Given also that cohesiveness is expressed in terms of the affective, non-instrumental behaviour of the group, it is easy to see why such group exercises focus on the release of emotional tension, the breakdown of defences against learning, the enhancement of interaction among group members, and so on. The value of working towards such goals is unquestionable. However, some of the exercises and techniques recommended in training manuals and practised in countless training and adult education workshops are of questionable value. The 'ice-breaker', for example, is a familiar experience for most people involved in adult education. Like many experiential group techniques in adult education, its origins can be traced to the human potential movement and the techniques associated with it, such as 'T-groups' and 'encounter' groups. Some of the excesses of this movement have been documented by Malcolm (1975), who notes three key features of the exercises commonly used:

1 A focus on the immediate 'here-and-now' experience of participants.
2 A belief that individual change occurs more readily in groups.
3 A belief in the value of open, honest feedback and self-disclosure.

Malcolm's objection to these (exclusively) experiential exercises is that the individual, far from being enhanced, must surrender to the group will. In the typical T-group, which is an unstructured, essentially leaderless group which has as its purpose a fuller understanding of self and others, the rules governing the behaviour of participants are well known before-hand (despite disclaimers to the contrary). On Malcolm's account these rules operate very much against the individual. For example, the need to focus on the 'here and now' typically appears as an aggressive anti-intellectual attitude in the group, where the display of individual know-ledge and expertise is invariably interpreted as a defence against the spontaneous expression of feelings. Those behaviours which are en-couraged are those which are prohibited in the course of normal social interaction, at least in the adult population. Failure to accept 'honest' and 'open' feedback (which might mean some kind of abuse from another group member) is considered deviant, as is the failure to 'confess' one's true feelings, or worse still – not agreeing to participate in the activities of the group.

Malcolm makes a compelling case that the extreme elements of the human potential movement use techniques which are manipulative, demeaning and, because they are effective, quite dangerous. His case can also be applied to some experiential techniques adopted by adult edu-cators, particularly those used as short-cuts to establishing group cohesive-ness such as the 'icebreaker'. The typical icebreaker has all the ingredients of the human potential 'experiential' exercise: it often involves some kind of childish game, it invariably requires group interaction on an emotional level, and it demands some kind of self-disclosure. The following is one of twenty-one icebreakers recommended in *More Games Trainers Play* by Edward Scannell and John Newstrom (1983); it is called the 'Magic Circle':

> Divide the group into teams of five–seven people. If possible, arrange the chairs in a circular fashion. On a prepared set of 3" × 5" cards, a series of words or phrases are written (one on each card, e.g. motivation; put-down; I feel good when . . .). The group leader pulls a card at random and each person is asked to state what the word means to them, or in the case of sentence completion, continue the statement. Continue for five–seven minutes for each card.
>
> (Scannell and Newstrom 1983: 19)

This exercise amounts to a public display of free association among the members of the group who are meeting, presumably, for the first time. The discussion question recommended is 'What barriers to communication did the exercise show?' The progress of this exercise would very much depend on how it was introduced and the 'climate setting' of the leader prior to introducing it. However, it is a risky exercise, and one can imagine all manner of disastrous outcomes. One option for participants is to treat the exercise in a light-hearted fashion and play along with the game of 'confessing' one's barriers to communication. But the more likely scenario here is that participants will play the game according to different rules and those who choose to take it seriously (with genuine self-disclosure) will be at risk.

For the most part icebreakers are harmless games which, at the very worst, may be a little insulting to the participants' intelligence or capacity for social intercourse. But one should nevertheless be conscious of the dangers of using such exercises at the beginning of the group life. The individual at this point is likely to be more compliant and it is particularly difficult to opt for non-participation. There are, however, three funda-mental principles in using group experiential techniques, which, if properly adhered to, will reduce the possibility of a harmful group experience and enhance the possibility of learning. These are:

1 The principle of informed consent, i.e. the participants should be told precisely the nature of the exercise.
2 The principle of freedom to participate, i.e. the participants should be free to leave the group at any time. Ideally this freedom means freedom from the group pressure to conform, which of course is something extremely difficult to eliminate. It is therefore a principle which needs to be strongly stated and frequently reiterated by the group facilitator.
3 The principle of critical reflection, i.e. making sense of the experience by analysing and evaluating it (see Boud *et al.* 1985; Zeichner and Liston 1987).

A particularly insidious practice is to manipulate the group solely for the purpose of building cohesion and commitment. The following advice, written by an influential and respected academic, serves as a warning to us all:

Some of the procedures used in communes to create such commitments can be employed in community groups as well. First of all the entity is separated from other groups. Within this isolated body, officials use special methods to shape the members' values and actions. . . . In one of these procedures, called *sacrifice*, a participant is asked to give up valued behaviors or objects, on the assumption that the strength of his or her desire to remain within the entity increases once the individual has agreed to abandon precious possessions for the cause. Another mechanism, labeled *renunciation*, requires a participant to renounce all relationships with persons outside the commune, in order to heighten closeness with those on the inside. The members are told to shun contacts with friends, relatives, and other non-members and are forbidden to leave the grounds.

(Zander 1990: 84–5)

The disturbing thing is that this advice is offered in an otherwise excellent treatment of how community groups can be harnessed for social action!

Earlier I argued that a great deal of group work in adult education is done in the name of individual growth and development. Paradoxically, one of the greatest dangers of group work comes from the power of the group to shape and maintain the behaviour and beliefs of its members. In this context a knowledge of group dynamics can best be used to ward off oppressive aspects of the group. This is a particularly important function for adult educators who constantly witness the transformation of collections of individuals into groups of one sort or another.

MEETING THE NEEDS OF THE GROUP

Groups are often seen as vehicles for enhancing learner participation in programme planning: the belief is that it is only through group methods that the true needs of the group can be expressed. The idea of meeting needs, however, is not as straightforward as it initially sounds. There are those who reject the needs-meeting paradigm as a legitimate approach to adult education provision (e.g. Armstrong 1982; Griffin 1983), claiming that it is no more than a slogan which serves only the interests of the professional providers. These commentators generally focus on the ideological workings of the needs concept and how it influences the broad sweep of adult education provision. But my concern here is with what 'needs meeting' means for an adult educator who is confronted with a group of learners and who has some notion that meeting their needs might be a good idea. The first difficulty this person will face is to distinguish between the needs, demands and wants of the group (see Wiltshire 1973; Lawson 1975; Tennant 1985b). Wants are normally considered to be desires, pure and simple, without any appraisal of the value of satisfying those desires. A demand is conceived as the overt expression of a want; 'We would like to learn some fundamental theorems' or 'We want more time allocated to class discussion' are examples of direct demands. An indirect demand would be the number of people who drop out of the course; as Newman has remarked: 'Having no one turn up concentrates the adult educator's mind wonderfully' (1979: 147). A need then is a 'want' or 'demand' which is deemed worthy of satisfying. Thus needs are not neutral: they require a judgement by someone about the relative merits of satisfying different wants or demands. Exactly how this judgement is to be made in a learning group is indeed problematic.

This scenario is further complicated by the contradiction of trying to meet both individual and group needs simultaneously. To assume that group needs are compatible with the interests of individual members presupposes a consensus which is rarely evident. Indeed, there is a necessary gap between the needs and interests of the group and the needs and interests of the individual. Every group at some stage infringes on individual autonomy and therefore a judgement must be made about a just or equitable arrangement for meeting the needs of the individual in the context of the group's needs.

One technique, the Nominal Group Technique (NGT), is arguably a good way to approach the two tasks of evaluating wants/demands and blending individual and group needs. The steps in this technique are outlined in Table 8.1.

This technique has been designed to allow a balanced input from all group members, especially during the initial stages. It also preserves the anonymity of the voter, thereby (presumably) reducing the pressure on the individual to conform to majority opinion. But it is a mechanical process which really only delays the issue at stake: what to do with the final list of ideas. Is the final list of ideas binding on all members of the group? Is it subject to revision? What are the conditions under which it can be revised? These questions indicate that in the NGT, the neutrality of the seminar leader and the diminution of the group dynamics process are short lived. Sooner or later the group must start functioning as a group and not as a mechanical device for meeting needs or decision making.

Table 8.1 Steps in the Nominal Group Technique

1	The task is stated (e.g. what issues should this series of seminars address?).
2	Participants write down their ideas silently and independently.
3	All ideas are listed in 'round-robin' fashion with clarifying comments/ questions but no discussion.
4	Ideas are defended by the proposer and agreements or disagreements are voiced.
5	Group members evaluate the ideas, list their top five priorities and then rank these priorities from highest (5 points) to lowest (1 point).
6	The vote is tallied and the results recorded on a flowchart.
7	There is further discussion of the ideas and the voting pattern.
8	The voting process is repeated, the ideas are tallied and then listed in rank order.

There are many other techniques comparable to the NGT but they mostly amount to a set of rules for decision making or problem solving which function in a similar manner to 'standing orders' in a committee meeting. But this is rarely the most fruitful way to proceed in establishing group needs. The idea that a group 'need' is there at the start of a learning process is a mistaken one. Most adult learning groups are artificial in the sense that it is individuals who come to learn and the group emerges only when there is a recognition of interdependence. Using a mechanical technique at the outset as a method of programme planning will result only in an aggregation of individual needs; it will almost certainly fail to register the needs arising from the emerging interdependence within the group.

GROUP DEVELOPMENT

The brief examples of group techniques in this chapter could be multiplied. The point I wish to draw from them is that groups are not mechanical objects which can be manipulated by a skilled facilitator.

The literature on group development confirms this view. In general it considers groups to be organic entities with characteristic and predictable patterns of growth and development. Jaques (see Table 8.2) summarises and tabulates twelve approaches to describing group development. An inspection of this table reveals that they all identify between three and six 'stages' or 'phases' in group life, which are typically described in terms of how the group sorts out its authority, power and interpersonal relationships. Tuckman and Jensen's (1977) analysis portrays in a simple manner the principal features of this literature. They describe groups as moving through these stages:

1 Forming – where there is anxiety, dependence on a leader, and testing to find out the nature of the situation and what behaviour is acceptable.
2 Storming – where there is a conflict between sub-groups, rebellion against the leader, a polarisation of opinions, and emotional resistance to the demands of the task.
3 Norming – where norms emerge and there is a development of an open exchange of views and feelings.
4 Performing – where interpersonal problems are resolved and there are constructive attempts to complete the task.
5 Adjourning – where tasks are completed and roles are terminated accompanied by a reduction in dependency and a degree of emotionality

(Tuckman and Jensen 1977)

This development process has much in common with the life span developmental theories discussed earlier: there is a linear, step-by-step progression from immaturity to maturity which occurs across a range of group types (natural groups, laboratory groups, training groups, therapy groups etc.). Some approaches extend the parallel with individual life span development one step further and include the decline and death of the group (e.g. Mills 1964; Mann 1967; Dunphy 1968). Others minimise the linear-progressive aspects of group development and emphasise instead the recurring nature of the 'phases' or 'stages'; of group life (e.g. Bion 1968; Schutz 1955).

Most adult educators who work with groups have a sense of the evolution of group identity and the fluctuations in group life which accompany this process. The group development literature is useful in that it helps the adult educator to interpret events occurring within the group. However, it is unclear how the adult educator would respond to these events and intervene in the group process. The option most frequently discussed in the literature is to devise strategies for facilitating the group through its various phases. In this role the adult educator operates rather like a lubricant in a motor car – it ensures a smoothly functioning process but has no regard for direction and destination. This role is appropriate only where the group is genuinely free to pursue its own course, but this is rarely the case and most adult learning groups function within non-negotiable parameters and constraints. A fatal mistake in organising any adult learning group is to create an illusion of freedom in the group which in fact does not exist. For example an orientation programme for a group of adult learners may be organised around their perceptions of what they want to learn and how they intend to accomplish their goals. The organisers may have designed the orientation to facilitate the process of group development. They may be putting into practice Bennis and Shepard's (1956) recommendation that at the first stage of group development the organiser should abnegate the traditional role of structuring the situation, setting up the rules of play and so on. When this illusion of freedom is shattered and the external constraints are made explicit, the organisers may interpret the subsequent hostility of the group towards them as simply indicating the next phase of group development (disenthrallment with organisers). However, this would be trivialising what would be more accurately interpreted as a predictable response to being deceived.

The point emerging from the above hypothetical scenario is that group events need to be interpreted in terms of the context in which the group exists. Groups do not operate in a vacuum with their own internal logic and developmental timetable. The dynamics of a group reflect not only its level of maturity, but also the external constraints operating on it. A change in these external constraints can have an effect on group dynamics which overrides any ongoing developmental process. To this extent, any notion of group maturity is at best provisional.

To conclude, much of the applied group dynamics literature places too much emphasis on the skills of the group facilitator and too little emphasis on how a knowledge of group dynamics can be used to empower the group. Notwithstanding this, most adult educators would acknowledge the importance of building a good climate for learning and fostering connections among the students. This may require a temporary suspension of critical thought and analysis while the group explores their feelings

Table 8.2 Some approaches to group development

Thelen and Dickerman (1949)	*Phase 1* Individually centred	*Phase 2* Frustration and conflict	*Phase 3* Attempted consolidation of group harmony	*Phase 4* Individual self-assessment, flexibility of group process, emphasis upon productivity in problem solving	
Miles (1955)	*Phase 1* Unoriented, restive 'talking about' irrelevant matters	*Phase 2* Abstract 'talking about' leadership and permissiveness	*Phase 3* 'Doing level' – discussion and analysis of here-and-now		
Bennis and Shepard (1956)	*Subphase 1* Dependence-submission	*Subphase 2* Counter-dependence	*Subphase 3* Resolution	*Subphase 4* Enchantment	*Subphase 5* Disenchantment
	Phase 1 Dependence				*Subphase 6* Conceptual validation
				Phase 2 Interdependence	
Bion (1990)	*Stage 1* Flight	*Stage 2* Fight		*Stage 3* Unite	
Golembiewski (1962)	*Phase 1* Establishing the hierarchy	*Phase 2* Conflict and frustration	*Phase 3* Growth of security and autonomy	*Phase 4* Structuring in terms of work task	
Bradford et al. (1964)	*Stage 1* Ambiguity	*Stage 2* Self-investment and participation	*Stage 3* Collaboration and learning from peers	*Stage 4* Motivation for learning	*Stage 5* Experienced behaviour and feedback
					Stage 6 Group growth and development
Mills (1964)	*Stage 1* The encounter	*Stage 2* Testing boundaries and modelling behaviour	*Stage 3* Negotiating and indigenous normative system	*Stage 4* Production	*Stage 5* Separation

Source	Stage 1 / Phase 1	Stage 2 / Phase 2	Stage 3 / Phase 3	Phase 4 / Stage 4	Stage 5 / Phases 5 & 6
Tuckman (1965)	*Stage 1* Forming – testing and dependence	*Stage 2* Storming – intragroup conflict	*Stage 3* Norming – development of group cohesion	*Stage 4* Performing – functional role relatedness	
Mann (1967)	*Phase 1* Initial complaining	*Phase 2* Premature enactment	*Phase 3* Confrontation	*Phase 4* Internalisation	*Phases 5 & 6* Separation and terminal review
Dunphy (1968)	*Phase 1 Phase 2 Phase 3* Counterpersonal and negativity; Maintenance of external normative standard	Individual rivalry and aggression	*Phase 4* Transitional – negativity membership	Realisation of unattainable Utopian ideals	*Phase 5s* Emotional concerns; *Phase 6* End of group
Tuckman and Jensen (1977)	*Stage 1* Forming	*Stage 2* Storming	*Stage 3* Norming	*Stage 4* Performing	*Stage 5* Adjourning
Napier and Gershenfeld (1981)	*Stage 1* Beginning – hesitation and testing	*Stage 2* Movement towards confrontation	*Stage 3* Compromise and harmony	*Stage 4* Reassessment – union of emotional and task components	*Stage 5* Resolution and recycling

Source: adapted from Jaques (1992: 38–9)

and expresses their concerns. It is at these moments that the group facilitator thrives – as a director of the process, but not the content. A highly cohesive and consensual group, however, should never be seen as an end in itself: there are always the broader questions to be considered such as 'cohesion for what purpose?' and 'cohesion at what price?' – questions which are often overlooked by that skilled adult learning technician, the group facilitator.

Chapter 9

Critical awareness

Myles Horton, the lay preacher who established the Highlander Folk School in Tennessee in the 1930s, once remarked 'An unanalysed experience is a kind of a happening' (Horton 1986). When he made this remark he was leading a seminar on his work at Highlander and he was being questioned about his approach to teaching and learning. He observed that the people with whom he worked – the poor, blacks, labour groups – had never been encouraged to analyse their experiences. His approach was to build programmes based on real problems, help groups analyse their collective experiences of those problems and encourage some form of collective action to bring about social change (see Adams 1975). The idea of analysing one's experiences to achieve liberation from psychological repression (e.g. psychoanalysis) or social and political oppression is a recurring theme in adult education. It is most commonly identified with the work of Freire (1972, 1974) but it is also a feature of some contemporary conceptions of self-directed learning (Brookfield 1985a), andragogy (Mezirow 1983), action research (Carr and Kemmis 1983; Kemmis 1985), models of the learning process (Jarvis 1987a, 1992) and techniques of facilitation (Boud *et al.* 1985; Boud 1987).

Freire (1974) adopts the term 'conscientisation' to describe the process whereby people come to understand that their view of the world and their place in it (their consciousness) is shaped by social and historical forces which work against their own interests. 'Conscientisation' leads to a critical awareness of the self as a subject who can reflect and act upon the world in order to transform it. Freire applied his ideas while working with literacy programmes in Brazil in the early 1960s:

> From the beginning, we rejected the hypothesis of a purely mechanistic literacy program and considered the problem of teaching adults how to read in relation to the awakening of their consciousness. We wished to design a project in which we would attempt to move from naïveté to a critical attitude at the same time we taught reading. We wanted a literacy program which would be an introduction to the democratization of

culture, a program with men as its subjects rather than as patient recipients. . . . The more accurately men grasp true causality, the more critical their understanding of reality will be. Their understanding will be magical to the degree that they fail to grasp causality. Further, critical consciousness always submits that causality to analysis; what is true today may not be so tomorrow. Naive consciousness sees causality as a static, established fact, and thus is deceived in its perception.

(Freire 1974: 43–4)

Freire argues that oppressed and subjugated people lack a critical understanding of their reality. To them, the world is something which is fixed and to which they must adapt. This view is supported by an oppressive social structure which has a vested interest in objectifying the world, making all aspects of a person's situation appear 'natural' and therefore unalterable. The first step towards critical understanding is to appreciate the distinction between the world of nature (which is unalterable) and the world of culture (which is a social construction and thereby alterable). Figure 9.1 is a reproduction of a drawing which Freire used with a literacy discussion group or 'culture circle'.

The group co-ordinator initiates the debate by distinguishing between culture and nature in the situation which is depicted. For example, the participants make a distinction between the feathers of the bird as nature

Figure 9.1 An illustration used by Freire
Source: Freire (1974: 66)

or culture. While the feathers are on the bird they belong to the world of nature, after the bird is killed and the feathers are transformed into decorative headware, they belong to the world of culture. The 'culture circle' discusses a variety of pictorially represented situations such as these, always with an emphasis on how culture is created and transmitted and on the possibility of democratising culture.

> Literacy makes sense only in these terms, as the consequence of men's beginning to reflect about their own capacity for reflection, about the world, about their position in the world, about their work, about their power to transform the world, about the encounter of consciousness – about literacy itself, which thereby ceases to be something external and becomes a part of them, comes as a creation from within them. I can see validity only in a literacy program in which men understand words in their true significance: as a force to transform the world. As illiterate men discover the relativity of ignorance and of wisdom, they destroy one of the myths by which false elites have manipulated them.
>
> (Freire 1974: 81)

Appreciating the distinction between nature and culture in the context of learning to read and write constitutes a basis for problematising previously taken-for-granted aspects of everyday life. Problems such as housing, clothing, diet, health, education and so on are now seen as problems which can be transformed by democratisation.

Horton and Freire have many things in common; they both believe in the liberating potential of education, especially when the critical analysis of experience is linked with action upon the world to transform it. They both work with disadvantaged and oppressed groups and their methods are overtly politicising. Naturally, their political activities sparked a reaction from those with an interest in maintaining the status quo: Freire was sent into exile and Highlander was repeatedly attacked by the Ku Klux Klan and eventually its charter was revoked by the State of Tennessee (it continued to operate under a new charter).

Adult educators frequently question the relevance of Freire to the circumstances of non-disadvantaged groups. However, Freire certainly considered dominant groups to be oppressed, at least in the psychological sense of having inauthentic personal identities – inauthentic in that they have become agents of oppression. This gives them a dual status as both dominators and dominated. Freire writes about the well-intentioned professionals who discover the violence of their acts of invasion: 'Those who make this discovery face a difficult alternative: they feel the need to renounce invasion, but patterns of domination are so entrenched within them that this renunciation would become a threat to their own identities' (1972: 125). This can be illustrated by considering the response of men to women's demands for equality in the workplace. Many male professionals have recently taken an interest in understanding the 'world view' of women. Now this can be done in the interests of domination, in which case the male professionals would learn 'about' women, or in the interests of liberation, where the male professionals would develop a critical awareness of the dynamics of gender identity. There are many instances like this in adult education and training, that is, where there is a clear choice between critical understanding, where the 'knower' is implicated in the situation, and a purely technical understanding, where the 'knower' remains detached from the situation and maintains the posture of an onlooker.

Indeed, this is a central issue in adult education and it has a direct bearing on how we conceive the ideal adult learner. Both Brookfield and Mezirow, for example, have re-formulated earlier conceptualisations of the self-directed learner to include the idea of critical awareness.

Mezirow has his own version of 'conscientisation': he refers to a similar process labelled 'perspective transformation' which is

> the emancipatory process of becoming critically aware of how and why the structure of psycho-cultural assumptions has come to constrain the way we see ourselves and our relationships, reconstituting this structure to permit a more inclusive and discriminating integration of experience and acting upon these new understandings. It is the learning process by which adults come to recognise their culturally induced dependency roles and relationships and the reasons for them and take action to overcome them.
>
> (Mezirow 1983: 125)

Later he links this process with a re-formulation of the concept of andragogy (Table 9.1).

It is worth comparing his 'Charter for andragogy' with Knowles' distinction between andragogy and pedagogy. Mezirow's 'Charter' specifies a set of precepts for adult educators which are targeted at fostering self-direction. However, this is self-direction with a new complexion: it includes the idea of critical awareness. A mature, self-directed learner is able to make a commitment to learning on the basis of a knowledge of genuine alternatives. Critically aware learners are in touch with their authentic needs – a characteristic which, incidentally, makes the adult educator's task so much easier because the problematic of meeting needs (as discussed earlier) evaporates.

Brookfield follows a similar line in exploring the concept of self-directedness when he emphasises the importance of learners appreciating the contextuality of knowledge and being aware of the culturally constructed nature of values, belief systems and moral codes. Self-direction is the capacity to critically reflect on this and to explore alternative perspectives and meaning systems (see Brookfield 1985a: 15).

Table 9.1 Mezirow's charter for andragogy

1 Progressively decrease the learner's dependency on the educator.
2 Help the learner to understand how to use learning resources – especially the experience of others, including the educator, and how to engage others in reciprocal learning relationships.
3 Assist the learner to define his or her learning needs – both in terms of immediate awareness and of understanding the cultural and psychological assumptions influencing his or her perceptions of needs.
4 Assist learners to assume increasing responsibility for defining their learning objectives, planning their own learning programme and evaluating their progress.
5 Organise what is to be learned in relationship to his or her current personal problems, concerns and levels of understanding.
6 Foster learner decision making/select learner-relevant learning experiences which require choosing, expand the learner's range of options, facilitate taking the perspectives of others who have alternative ways of understanding.
7 Encourage the use of criteria for judging which are increasingly inclusive and differentiating in awareness, self-reflexive and integrative of experience.
8 Foster a self-corrective reflexive approach to learning – to typifying and labelling, to perspective taking and choosing, and to habits of learning and learning relationships.
9 Facilitate problem posing and problem solving, including problems associated with the implementation of individual and collective action; recognition of relationships between personal problems and public issues.
10 Reinforce the self concept of the learner as a learner and doer by providing for progressive mastery; a supportive climate with feedback to encourage provisional efforts to change and to take risks; avoidance of competitive judgement of performance; appropriate use of mutual support groups.
11 Emphasize experiential, participative and projective instructional methods; appropriate use of modelling and learning contracts.
12 Make the moral distinction between helping the learner understand his or her full range of choices and how to improve the quality of choosing vs encouraging the learner to make a specific choice.

Source: Mezirow (1983: 136–7)

In a later publication Brookfield (1994) specifically singles out critical reflection and critical thinking as the hallmark of his and his colleagues' work at Columbia University Teachers College, and goes on to define what is meant by critical reflection in the context of documenting the process among adult educators:

In an act of rhetorical optimism, and perhaps terminal naivety, the development of critical thinking and critical reflection has been advanced by several writers associated with Columbia University Teachers College as the organising concept to inform adult education practice . . . the form of critical reflection explored is defined as comprising three interrelated processes: (1) the experience of questioning and then replacing or reframing an assumption or assumptive cluster, which is unquestioningly accepted as representing dominant common sense by a majority; (2) the experience of taking a perspective on social and political structures, or on personal and collective actions, which is strongly alternative to that held by a majority; (3) the experience of studying the ways in which ideas, and their representations in actions and structures, are accepted as self evident renderings of the 'natural' state of affairs.

(Brookfield 1994: 203–4)

Both Brookfield and Mezirow have introduced a social dimension to the concept of self-directed learning. They admit that there are constraints on learning which originate in the social structure and which become internalised by the learner. This is their point of contact with the more radical adult educators such as Freire (1972), Gelpi (1979), Griffin (1983) and Lovett *et al.* (1983) and it separates them quite sharply from the humanistic point of view. By way of summary, Table 9.2 contrasts the critical awareness and humanistic traditions in terms of their stance on a number of key adult education issues: the nature of self-directed learning, needs-based provision, equity and access, and the relationship between teachers and learners.

There is something incomplete about Brookfield and Mezirow's analysis of critical awareness. The reason, I think, is that they have depoliticised the idea. They focus inwardly, as it were, on the liberation of the learner and they very much stand on the fence when it comes to organising collective actions. This point has been made repeatedly in a number of publications and has generated lively debate, especially with respect to Mezirow (see Clark and Wilson 1991; Mezirow 1991b; Mezirow 1992; Newman 1993; Tennant 1993; Mezirow 1994). Despite Mezirow's protestations, he still maintains the view that his theory of learning is distanced from action:

A learning theory attempts to describe an abstract, idealized model, the elements and dynamics of which may or may not be applied in a variety of social and educational settings.... Transformations in learning may occur in or out of a social action context.... Reflective action may or may not involve some form of social action.

(Mezirow 1994: 231–2)

However, Freire argues that an unmasking of reality needs to be followed by critical intervention in order to transform it. For him, thought and action are indissoluble aspects of a single dialectical process (praxis). 'Mere reflection is nothing but verbalism. It becomes an empty word, one which cannot denounce the world, for denunciation is impossible without a commitment to transform, and there is no transformation without action' (Freire 1972: 61). By way of contrast, pure action without reflection is nothing but activism – action for its own sake, which prevents dialogue and liberation.

Table 9.2 Contrasting traditions in the framing of issues in adult education

	Self-directed learning	Needs-based provision	Equity and access	Teacher–learner relationship
Humanistic tradition	This occurs when learners determine goals and objectives, locate appropriate resources, plan their learning strategies and evaluate the outcomes. It is the appropriate way for mature adults to learn. It ensures freedom, autonomy, independence, student centredness and relevance. Learning is the responsibility of the learner: no one can learn for someone else.	Adult educators have a responsibility to meet the expressed needs of learners. These can be identified in a variety of ways: through responses to course offerings, group discussions, questionnaires, local government statistics, student planning committees, etc. It is the responsibility of individuals and groups of individuals to express their needs.	Adult education is characterised by open access to courses. Management structures and administrative practices ensure that access is guaranteed for those who seek it. It is the responsibility of the individual to exercise his or her right to learn as an adult.	The teacher is a 'facilitator' of learning. This means having empathy with and trust in the learner, being genuine with the learner, and being open, caring and non-judgemental. This enables the learner to express his or her needs and it ensures that the larger group overcomes its conflicts. Here, learning is premised on individual freedom.
Critical awareness tradition	Autonomy and freedom is not to be found in the mastery of techniques and procedures for self-learning. Much of the literature documenting self-directed learning is questionable on the grounds of its middle-class bias, both because of the populations surveyed and the nature of the survey and interview techniques. Self-direction should include the element of critical awareness of the social and cultural constraints impinging on one's behaviour.	The expressed needs of learners may have nothing at all to do with the objective educational needs of a group or community. Learners and potential learners are not always in a position to articulate their needs and thus may be unaware of the range of possibilities from which to choose. The needs-meeting paradigm is an aspect of the free market approach and it contains all the social and political trappings that go with it.	An educational provision which relies on self-selection will widen, not narrow, educational and cultural gaps in society. Research on participation in adult education shows consistently that students are young, middle class and well educated. Adult education institutions need to actively recruit non-traditional students if the goal of equity is to be realised. They need to identify the social and cultural barriers to participation.	The teacher and learner enter a dialogue based on mutual trust. However, the teacher plays an active role in challenging the learner's presuppositions – and confusion, uncertainty and ambiguity may result. Teaching and learning is a collaborative enterprise and the teacher does not have a monopoly on the right to challenge and intervene.

Whether or not one subscribes to Freire's position, there is nevertheless a sense in which Brookfield and Mezirow fail to address the issue of action following from critical awareness. There is an implicit liberal tradition in their writing; that more perceptive and better educated (in their sense) individuals magically produce a more just and equitable society.

The relationship between critical awareness and action has been foregrounded elsewhere – in the domain of adult education research. Participatory or action research has been actively sponsored by adult education agencies such as the International Council for Adult Education (ICAE). The impetus for this has come partly from a sense of disquiet about research techniques which mimic the procedures of physical science (i.e. experimental control, hypothetico-deductive method) and partly from a political commitment to popular involvement in social research. The thrust of the ICAE's project is to link social and educational research to economic and social development, particularly in the Third World. One aspect of the project is to develop a view about how best to approach social and educational inquiry. Carr and Kemmis (1983), although working quite independently of the ICAE project, have sketched a scenario for research which has as its core the fusion of critical awareness and action. Their version of critical awareness has much in common with that of Brookfield and Mezirow, but they proceed a step further and explore the research implications of a commitment to the idea of being critically aware.

Carr and Kemmis (1983) and Mezirow (1983) adopt a common starting point in using Habermas' (1972) distinction between instrumental, practical and emancipatory knowledge. Instrumental knowledge allows us to control the environment. It is the type of knowledge which is commonly generated by empirical-analytic or natural sciences, where the researcher is an objective observer whose task is to identify cause–effect relationships. Practical knowledge helps us to understand the environment. It does so by providing interpretations of actions and events which can inform and guide our practical judgement. Emancipatory knowledge helps us to break free from the taken-for-granted assumptions which guide our everyday behaviours and which distort our self-understanding. This type of knowledge is formed through a critique of the historical and social forces which shape our consciousness. It is this type of critique which Freire encouraged in his culture circles. It is also a characteristic of the critical social sciences (e.g. Marx's theory of society and Freud's metapsychology) and it is advocated by Carr and Kemmis as the basis for emancipatory action research.

Carr and Kemmis set out to provide a rationale of the view that educational research should be construed as a form of critical social science where teachers are researchers in the sense that they systematically reflect on their practice. Their reflection, of course, must be 'critical':

It must provide ways of distinguishing ideas and interpretations which are systematically distorted by ideology from those which are not, and provide a view of how distorted self-understandings can be overcome.

It must be concerned to identify and expose those aspects of the existing social order which frustrate rational change, and must be able to offer theoretical accounts which enable teachers (and other participants) to become aware of how they may be overcome.

(Carr and Kemmis 1983: 158)

The notion of 'critical' reflection is a key one for Carr and Kemmis and they proceed to demonstrate how the method they propose ensures a critical perspective. Their method, somewhat disappointingly, turns out to be remarkably simple: it consists of the notion of a spiral of self-reflection:

- to develop a plan of action to improve what is already happening,
- to act to implement the plan,
- to observe the effects of action in the context in which it occurs, and
- to reflect on these effects as a basis for further planning, subsequent action and so on, through a succession of cycles.

(Kemmis and McTaggart 1982: 7)

The Action Research Planner, developed by Kemmis and McTaggart (1982), details the sequence of steps in the action research spiral; it is essentially a checklist of what to do when carrying out action research. It is certainly useful as a basis for reflecting on practice, and it definitely encourages a critical attitude towards practice, but there is a notable gap between the promise of social and political enlightenment and the rather mundane advice to attend to questions like 'What is happening now?' 'In what sense is this problematic?' 'Who is affected?' 'With whom must I negotiate?' 'Am I reflecting on the issues?' 'What rethinking of the general idea or problem is called for?'

Carr and Kemmis advance an elegant and sophisticated rationale for emancipatory action research. Ultimately, however, they are caught in the same void as Habermas – between the idea of a critical social and educational science and its concrete realisation. The Action Research Planner constitutes an attempt to give concrete expression to the actions carried out by action researchers – but the steps and procedures to be followed are general, designed to fit almost any teaching situation. The point is that it is not possible to know in advance whether the recommended steps will or will not lead to a critique of a given situation and a commitment to improve it. Action research as a method is not (as Carr and Kemmis claim) intrinsically critical.

There is a general tendency among advocates of the 'critical awareness' approach to emphasise the importance of method and procedure at the expense of content and direction (this does not apply to Horton). For example, Freire's distinction between banking education and problem-posing education is essentially a distinction between different methods of learning, one necessarily oppressive, the other necessarily liberating.

> Banking education (for obvious reason) attempts, by mythicizing reality, to conceal certain facts which explain the way men exist in the world; problem-posing education sets itself the task of de-mythologizing. Banking education resists dialogue; problem-posing education regards dialogue as indispensable to the act of cognition which unveils reality. Banking education treats students as objects of assistance; problem-posing education makes them critical thinkers. Banking education inhibits creativity and domesticates (although it cannot completely destroy) the intentionality of consciousness by isolating consciousness from the world, thereby denying men their ontological and historical vocation of becoming more fully human. Problem-posing education bases itself on creativity and stimulates true reflection and action upon reality, thereby responding to the vocation of men as beings who are authentic only when engaged in inquiry and creative transformation. In sum: banking theory and practice, as immobilizing and fixating forces, fail to acknowledge men as historical beings; problem-posing theory and practice take man's historicity as their starting point.
>
> (Freire 1972: 56)

Lovett *et al.* (1983) deny the validity of this distinction and claim that many features of so-called banking education (for example, that the teacher teaches and the students are taught) are not intrinsically oppressive at all. Furthermore Lovett defends the idea of vigorous, ordered and sustained schooling: 'education aiming to promote the eradication of class division must include, at the very least, some old-fashioned instruction, set into an ordered curriculum, which includes basic information and skills required to execute necessary management tasks' (1983: 145). Lovett challenges the critical awareness approach on two counts. First, that questions of pedagogic method are secondary, and that the overall purpose of the education is what really matters (i.e. the *content* of learning needs to fit the political aspirations of the learners). Second, that oppression does not simply evaporate through learners psychologically re-orienting themselves to the world (i.e. unmasking the myths upon which oppression is based). Lovett makes this last point forcefully in his reaction to the rhetoric of action research:

> Most of this is pure moralism: the liberation of more and more people's efforts is not the problem, since efforts are wasted without a macro-economic strategy that can co-ordinate them successfully, which is precisely what is lacking: the notion of a 'right' to create knowledge is

absurd unless it is qualified by some criteria distinguishing knowledge from error and allowing the construction of hierarchies of knowledge for the elaboration of theory; criteria, in other words, concerning the ability to create knowledge; and to hold that 'people can not be developed', is a rejection of the crucial determining role of education, at an individual level, and of macro-social change in human history – it is also, more importantly, false.

(Lovett *et al*. 1983: 109)

Lovett's case is quite compelling, the more so because of his well-documented activities with working-class communities. His concern is with the way in which adult learning, as a process which leads to critical awareness, is portrayed as a powerful force for social change. From the standpoint of a psychology of adult learning, 'critical awareness' is certainly a valuable outcome. However, it is a mistake to link this, as an outcome, with any particular method of learning. In particular, one should avoid the premature dissolution of the distinction between teachers and taught:

Teachers must avoid the kind of autocracy which undermines any democratic sensibility, but they must, nevertheless, teach and include in their teaching much of the best of what has been handed down by centuries of intellectual contest and co-operation.

(Lovett *et al*. 1983: 144)

This tension between pedagogical processes (techniques and methods) and pedagogical purposes and content (encompassing a vision of knowledge and education) is a recurring theme in debates about what counts as a critical emancipatory pedagogy (see, for example, Gore's (1993) analysis of the relationship between critical and feminist discourses). Clearly, adopting democratic techniques and processes is not sufficient for an emancipatory critical pedagogy; some attention to critical content is necessary, but the content must be grounded in teaching and learning situations, otherwise it can become isolated and isolating. But what is found in contemporary teaching and learning situations, even those explicitly designed to be emancipatory, is not the level of commonality among learners assumed by much of the critical awareness literature. Instead one finds difference and diversity. Arguably, attending to difference and diversity constitutes a new challenge for critical emancipatory pedagogy. Pietrykowski (1996), adopting a postmodern perspective, argues that grand narratives which promise an ideal emancipatory end state don't sufficiently acknowledge diversity and the multiple sources of power evident in everyday discourse. This is the thrust of the work of the New London Group who in 'A pedagogy of multiliteracies: designing social futures' (1996) portray a postmodern scenario of contemporary society characterised by civic pluralism and multiple life worlds:

The challenge is to make space available so that different lifeworlds –
spaces where local and specific meanings can be made – can flourish. . . .
As lifeworlds become more divergent in the new public spaces of civic
pluralism, their boundaries become more evidently complex and overlapping. . . . As people are simultaneously the members of multiple
lifeworlds, so their identities have multiple layers, that are in complex
relation to each other. No person is a member of a singular community,
rather they are members of multiple and overlapping communities –
communities of work, of interest and affiliation, of ethnicity, of gender,
and so on.

(New London Group 1996: 70–1)

They propose a pedagogy grounded in situated practice (gaining mastery
of practice), overt instruction (gaining conscious control and understanding), critical framing (gaining an understanding of the locatedness of
practice in history, culture and values), and transformed practice (return-
ing to practice in a more conscious and critical way). These elements are
readily identifiable in the literature prevously dealt with in this and earlier
chapters, but they do signal a concern with diversity, a strong connection
between method and content, and a commitment to the value of context.
As such their project is in a good position to address the dilemmas of
critical emancipatory pedagogy.

Chapter 10

Concluding comment

Psychology as a foundation discipline in adult education

Psychology is frequently used as a foundation discipline in the training of adult educators. This is because it addresses those questions which naturally emerge from an engagement with adult teaching and learning. What motivates students to attend classes? Through what processes do adults learn best? How can I adjust my teaching practices to take into account the learning styles of my students? How can I encourage the formation of a cohesive and supportive group? Can I make sense of the expressed anxieties and concerns of my students? What can I do to help those students who experience difficulties in learning? Much of the psychological literature has some bearing on each of these questions, and others like them. However, it is not at all clear how the practitioner should proceed to apply the output of this literature to the everyday activity of teaching adults. In this respect there appear to be at least three available options, each of them corresponding to a different motive within the practitioner: to control events in the learning environment, to interpret and influence events, or to gain a critical understanding of events and one's actions in relation to them.

CONTROL

The desire for control among adult educators (which is natural enough and quite understandable) is often linked with a particular view about the relationship between theory and practice. As a foundation discipline, psychology is viewed as providing a base of rules and principles which can be unequivocally applied to practice. The practitioner who holds such a view, however, is likely to be disappointed with what psychology can offer. The reasons for this have to do with the way in which 'scientific psychology' generates knowledge. As a science, psychology is very much concerned with prediction and control, and to this end seeks to identify cause–effect relationships. However, there are a number of factors which limit the direct practical application of such knowledge. First, psychological experiments which adopt the methods of natural science are characterised by what Egan (1984) calls 'phenomena insensitivity'. That is, while the methods are scientific, it may be at the cost of distorting and/or narrowing the phenomenon being investigated – so much that the results have little direct applicability outside the experimental context or the theoretical concerns of the experiment. This is an argument advanced by Usher (1986b) and it is neatly expressed in Harré's (1974) critique of social psychology:

> Psychologists have frequently supposed that one can divide up socially meaningful phenomena into basic non-meaningful units between which they have sought the kinds of correlations which Boyle and Hooke found between the pressures and volumes of gases. Let me give you an example. There have been studies of the development of liking between human beings. Psychologists have sought to investigate this process by identifying elementary features of the liking-generating process and studying them independently of all other features of a real situation of liking. They have isolated the frequency with which a person is confronted with another person as an element in the formation of liking between people. And then they have attempted to study the effect of frequency of meeting on the development of liking in an apparently 'pure' case. To this end, people were asked to report on the way in which their liking of nonsense syllables had changed with the frequency of presentation of such syllables.
>
> It should be clear that the most elementary examination of the social interaction which produces feelings of liking or disliking between people involves intimately and inextricably other elements besides mere frequency. Frequency is equivocal in social meaning. The notion of frequency by itself is not a social concept. It is an element which lacks the level of meaning at which liking and similar concepts apply.
>
> (Harré 1974: 249)

Of course, not all psychological experiments are open to such a challenge. Nevertheless, the problem of 'operationally' defining concepts like 'panic', 'obedience', 'conformity' and 'aggression', so that they can be measured in an experiment, is a factor limiting the generalisability and practical application of many research findings.

A related feature of psychological experiments is that they are conducted under controlled conditions. The experimenter achieves control either directly (which is the case with Skinner's laboratory experiments) or indirectly through, say, sampling techniques which select or randomise those variables which potentially confound the results. For example, an educational psychologist may be interested in plotting the effectiveness of a particular teaching strategy for subjects with different learning styles.

This could be accomplished by holding the teaching strategy constant across two groups composed of subjects who differed only in their learning styles (i.e. *not* differing on factors such as sex, age, intelligence, ethnic grouping). The aim would be to arrive at some statement such as 'Teaching strategy "X" is more effective for field-dependent people, all other things being equal'. A commonly perceived problem with applying this knowledge is that in everyday life 'all other things' are rarely, if ever, 'equal'. And in everyday life the extent of control is somewhat less than in a psychological experiment. But this misses the point – the very strength of a psychological experiment is its capacity to isolate variables for systematic study – and this means controlling other variables.

The position of psychology in this respect is not unique. For example, the laws and principles of other foundation disciplines such as physics or biology are characteristically qualified by an expression like 'all other things being constant'. And yet very few would deny the importance and relevance of physics and biology to the practices of engineering and medicine respectively. However, it *is* a mistake to assume that the knowledge derived from controlled experiments will necessarily lead to greater control of the environment.

A large component of the practitioner's skill consists of the ability to anticipate, recognise and compensate for the range of variables operating in a given context. Given this, the value of 'scientific psychology' becomes somewhat clearer. It is the corpus of experimental findings in a given area which identifies for the practitioner the range of likely variables operating and the subtleties of their interaction. This can be illustrated with reference to the corpus of research findings on the effectiveness of different teaching methods (see Gage 1976). If practitioners approach this literature looking for a set of generalisations to guide practice, they will invariably be frustrated. Nevertheless the literature is valuable in that it alerts practitioners to the range of variables influencing the effectiveness of a teaching method. In the first instance, whether or not a teaching method is effective will depend largely upon how 'effectiveness' is measured. There are a bevy of contenders here: motivation, recall, understanding, ability to learn, creativity, attitude change, etc. There are also different ways of measuring each of these factors. For example, attitude change can be measured using a questionnaire, interview, or some kind of behavioural index, and it can be measured immediately, in the short term, or over a longer period of time. In addition to these measurement variables there are a host of factors to consider such as the subject matter being taught, student ability, age, sex, ethnicity, the teacher's personality, size of class – all of which have been the focus of experimental inquiry. The value of this research is that it supplies the practitioner with a complex array of variables to consider when evaluating the appropriateness of a given teaching method in a given context. Used in this way psychology helps us to interpret and influence events in the learning environment, rather than control them.

INTERPRETATION AND INFLUENCE

Usher (1986b) advocates the application of therapy-derived theories to an understanding of adult teaching and learning. Unlike 'scientific' psychologies the approach of these theories is hermeneutic, that is, they seek to interpret behaviour and stimulate insight, awareness and understanding. Freudian psychoanalysis and humanistic clinical psychology (see Chapters 2 and 3) are examples of this type of theory. Usher argues that the activities of therapists and counsellors are more like the activities of teachers than are the experimental manipulations of the scientific psychologists. Both the therapist and the educator are concerned with interpreting on-going actions and events and adjusting their actions accordingly. Unlike the notions of 'prediction' and 'control', the terms 'interpretation' and 'influence' imply that the teacher (or therapist) is engaged in a reflexive dialogue with the student (or client). Thus the activity of teaching requires practical judgement in a context where the variables operating are unable to be measured or controlled. This practical judgement, and the action which flows from it, is informed by psychological theory in the sense that the theory provides a framework for interpreting events.

The difficulty with this model of the relationship between psychology and adult teaching and learning is that there exist competing theoretical frameworks which offer quite different interpretations of similar events. For example, an adult student may express disappointment with a course, claiming that it has failed to meet his or her need for a stimulating, exciting and challenging experience. A psychoanalytic interpretation may hold that such a demand is unrealistic, and is really an expression of an infantile wish to be totally loved and cared for unconditionally. A humanistic interpretation may hold that the same person is expressing a desire for growth and fulfilment, which is a natural and healthy thing to do. There are practitioners who remain undaunted by such opposing interpretations claiming that they operate by synthesising different theoretical perspectives, but Reese and Overton (1970), among others, have reservations about the possibility of this occurring:

> Theories built upon radically different models are logically independent and cannot be assimilated to each other. They reflect representations of different ways of looking at the world and as such are incompatible in their implications. Different world views involve different understanding of what is knowledge and hence of the meaning of truth. Therefore synthesis is at best confusing.
>
> (Reese and Overton 1970: 144)

One may remonstrate that practitioners are not bound by the rigours of theory construction in Reese and Overton's sense – and this is certainly true – but they do reflect upon or 'theorise' about their practice. That is, they form a relatively coherent 'world view' which informs their practical judgement. Such a 'world view' may be 'naive' or it may be more or less based upon a knowledge of psychology, philosophy or educational theory. A critical understanding of psychology can assist practitioners to re-examine the 'world view' they have adopted, to re-evaluate and re-formulate it. This was referred to earlier as a third option in linking psychology with adult teaching and learning.

CRITICAL UNDERSTANDING

There are two senses in which adult education practitioners can have a critical (psychological) understanding of their practice. The first sense has been outlined above: practitioners can interpret (rather than accept at face value) actions and events in the learning environment. In the second sense, practitioners can analyse the psychological 'world view' they adopt when interpreting those actions and events. This is where a critical under-standing of competing psychological theories is important, which means analysing the conceptual weaknesses and contradictions within each theory, evaluating whether each theory is supported by the evidence, assessing the success of the practices promoted by each theory, and finally, being aware of the social, historical and political origins and impact of each theory. By scrutinising their psychological world views, practitioners are better able to recognise and appreciate the world views of others and they are in a better position to articulate their goals and purposes as adult educators. There are many areas in adult education where a conflict of world views, especially between the teacher and student, is commonplace. I have in mind here areas such as literacy, numeracy, second language learning, worker education, 'second chance' education, education for unemployed people, health education, and so forth. In all of these areas there is a high probability that competing world views will emerge. Symptomatic of this will be differences in opinion among the students, or between the students and the teacher, about what constitutes relevant content, appropriate teaching methods, the role and responsibilities of the teacher, and the purposes of the programme.

While it is true that a commitment to a particular psychological 'world view' provides a powerful interpretive framework for adult educators, they need also to be aware of alternative 'world views'. A critical understanding of a range of psychological 'world views' is preferable to a blind faith in any single one. This does not mean that adult educators should adopt a chameleon-like character, shifting colours as the en-vironmental circumstances dictate; it means only that they should be aware of their 'world view' and understand its limitations in the context of the alternatives available.

A RECONSTRUCTED CHARTER FOR ANDRAGOGY

Although I am mindful of the criticisms which can be levelled against formulating generic guidelines for teachers, especially when they take the form of 'teachers should', 'teachers must' or 'teachers ought to' (see Gore 1993), I feel compelled at least to set out the characteristics of critical adult education practice which I have gleaned from the foregoing analysis. These characteristics are of course quite problematic and their meaning in specific contexts will differ, but they do provide an initial basis for framing practice. I have tried to decentre the teacher in setting out these characteristics, agreeing with Brookfield's observation that there is, rather ironically, an unnecessarily dichotomous conceptualisation of teacher and taught in much of the adult education literature (Brookfield 1993b).

Valuing the experiences of learners

This does not simply refer to an attitude towards other learners: attitudes are no guarantee that learners will feel valued. It implies that learners will feel comfortable that their life world is included in the teaching and learning discourse, and that they are equal and legitimate participants. This means that the materials, the language, the registers, the examples and the processes should be inclusive rather than exclusive.

Engaging in reflection on experiences

The aim here is to develop generalisations or frameworks for understanding experiences. Normally it is necessary to introduce new material and not rely solely on the existing experiences of participants. This is because the point of learning is not simply to confirm existing experiences, but is to go beyond experiences and, ironically, create a theoretical distance which allows generalisations to emerge.

Establishing collaborative learning relationships

The analysis of experience should not be solely an individual exercise. A prerequisite of truly collaborative group learning is the creation of diverse communities of learners who respect different life worlds: a willingness among learners to 'construe knowledge and values from multiple perspectives without loss of commitment to one's own values' (Bruner 1990: 30).

Addressing issues of identity and the power relationship between teachers and learners

The appropriate distribution of power will depend very much on the context. What is important is that the issue at least be addressed with a view to distributing as much power to the learners as seems warranted by the context.

Promoting judgements about learning which are developmental and which allow scope for success for all learners

Success should not be defined in terms of another's failure, or even in relation to the other, and assessments and judgements should be made with a view to further development.

Negotiating conflicts over claims to knowledge and pedagogical processes

The aim here is not necessarily to reach a consensus, but to allow the different points of view which exist in the group to emerge rather than be silent. It is to encourage learners to have a voice and to negotiate and engage critically with the material and the processes.

Identifying the historical and cultural locatedness of experiences

By this is meant the questioning of the taken-for-granted world and the social and cultural assumptions underlying one's experiences and their interpretation.

Transforming actions and practices

This refers to the implementation of new practices as a consequence of identifying the nature of one's historical and cultural locatedness. Although it is unlikely that individuals can substantially transcend their historical and cultural locatedness, there is some room to manoeuvre, and certainly actions can be changed, especially in concert with others.

This text has adopted a critical posture towards selected psychological theories and research findings. The purpose has not been to dissuade adult educators from further psychological inquiry, but to encourage them to approach their inquiry with a critical spirit. Approached in this way, psychological theory and research are better able to foster among adult educators a capacity for making informed choices which are defensible on rational, practical and moral grounds.

Bibliography

Adams, F. (1975) *Unearthing Seeds of Fire*, Charlotte, NC: Blair.

Alexander, C. N. and Langer, E. J. (eds) (1990) *Higher Stages of Human Development*, Oxford: Oxford University Press.

Allman, P. (1982) 'New perspectives on the adult: an argument for lifelong education', *International Journal of Lifelong Education* 1(1): 41–52.

Allport, G. (1961) *Pattern and Growth in Personality*, New York: Holt, Rinehart & Winston.

Anderson, J. A. (1988) 'Cognitive styles and multicultural populations', *Journal of Teacher Education* 39(1): 2–9.

Appel, M. H. and Goldberg, L. B. (eds) (1977) *Topics in Cognitive Development*, vol. 1, *Equilibration: Theory Research and Application*, New York: Plenum.

Appel, M. H., Presseisen, B. Z. and Goldstein, P. (eds) (1978) *Topics in Cognitive Development*, vol. 2, *Language and Operational Thought*, New York: Plenum.

Arlin, P. K. (1990) 'Wisdom: the art of problem finding', in R. J. Sternberg (ed.) *Wisdom: Its Nature, Origins, and Development*, Cambridge: Cambridge University Press.

Armistead, N. (ed.) (1974) *Reconstructing Social Psychology*, Harmondsworth: Penguin.

Armstrong, P. F. (1982) 'The needs meeting ideology in liberal adult education', *International Journal of Lifelong Education* 1(4): 293–321.

Asch, S. (1956) 'Studies of independence and conformity: a minority of one against a unanimous majority', *Psychological Monographs* 9 (complete volume).

Bales, R. (1950) *Interaction Process Analysis: A Method for the Study of Small Groups*, Cambridge, MA: Addison-Wesley.

Bales, R. (1958) 'Task roles and social roles in problem solving groups', in E. Maccoby, M. Newcomb and E. Hartley (eds) *Readings in Social Psychology*, New York: Holt, Rinehart & Winston.

Baltes, P. (1968) 'Longitudinal and cross-sectional sequences in the study of age and generation effects', *Human Development* 11: 145–71.

Baltes, P. B. (1987) 'Theoretical propositions of lifespan developmental psychology: on the dynamics between growth and decline', *Developmental Psychology* 23(5): 611–26.

Baltes, P. B. and Smith, J. (1990) 'Toward a psychology of wisdom and its ontogenesis', in R. J. Sternberg (ed.) *Wisdom: Its Nature, Origins, and Development*, Cambridge: Cambridge University Press.

Baltes, P. B., Dittman-Kohli, F. and Dixon, R. A. (1984) 'New perspectives on the development of intelligence in adulthood: toward a dual-process conception and a model of selective optimization with compensation', in P. B. Baltes and

O. G. Brim, Jr (eds) *Life-span Development and Behavior*, vol. 6 New York: Academic Press.

Bandura, A. (1969) *Principles of Behaviour Modification*, New York: Holt, Rinehart & Winston.

Basseches, M. (1984) *Dialectical Thinking and Adult Development*, Norwood, NJ: Ablex.

Basseches, M. (1986) 'Comments on social cognition in adulthood: a dialectical perspective', *Educational Gerontology* 12(4): 327–34.

Belenky, M., Clichy, B., Goldberger, N. and Tarule, J. (1986) *Women's Ways of Knowing: The Development of Self, Voice and Mind*, New York: Basic Books.

Bengtsson, J. (1979) 'The work/leisure/education life cycle', in T. Schuller and J. Megarry (eds) *Recurrent Education and Lifelong Learning*, London: Kogan Page.

Bennis, W. and Shepard, H. (1956) 'A theory of group development', *Human Relations* 9: 415–37.

Berger, P. and Luckmann, T. (1967) *The Social Construction of Reality*, Harmondsworth: Penguin.

Bion, W. (1968) *Experiences in Groups*, London: Tavistock.

Bion, W. (1990) *Experiences in Groups and Other Papers*, London: Routledge.

Bloom, B. (1956) *Taxonomy of Educational Objectives*, London: Longman.

Boucouvalas, M. (1988) 'An analysis and critique of the concept of self in self-directed learning: towards a more robust construct for research and practice', in M. Zukas (ed.) *Papers from the Transatlantic Dialogue*, Leeds: Standing Conference on University Teaching and Research in the Education of Adults.

Boud, D. (1981) *Developing Student Autonomy in Learning*, London: Kogan.

Boud, D. (1987) 'A facilitator's view of adult learning', in D. Boud and V. Griffin (eds) *Appreciating Adults Learning: From the Learner's Perspective*, London: Kogan Page.

Boud, D. and Walker, D. (1990) 'Making the most of experience', *Studies in Continuing Education* 12(2): 61–80.

Boud, D. and Walker, D. (1991) *Experience and Learning: Reflection at Work*, Geelong: Deakin University Press.

Boud, D., Keogh, R. and Walker, D. (eds) (1985) *Reflection: Turning Experience into Learning*, London: Kogan Page.

Boyer, D. (1984) 'Malcolm Knowles and Carl Rogers: a comparison of andragogy and student-centered education', *Lifelong Learning* 7(4): 17–20.

Bradford, L. (ed.) (1978) *Group Development*, La Jolla, CA: University Associates.

Bradford, L., Gibb, J. and Benne, K. (1964) *T-Group Theory and Laboratory Method: Innovation in Re-education*, New York: Wiley.

Braginsky, B. and Braginsky, D. (1974) *Mainstream Psychology: A Critique*, New York: Holt, Rinehart & Winston.

Brookfield, S. (1981) 'The adult learning iceberg: a critical review of the work of Allen Tough', *Adult Education* 54(2): 110–18.

Brookfield, S. (1983) *Adult Learners, Adult Education and the Community*, Milton Keynes: Open University Press.

Brookfield, S. (1985a) 'Self-directed learning: a critical review of research', in S. Brookfield (ed.) *Self-directed Learning: From Theory to Practice*, San Francisco: Jossey-Bass.

Brookfield, S. (1985b) 'A critical definition of adult education', *Adult Education Quarterly* 36(1): 44–9.

Brookfield, S. (1985c) 'Self-directed learning: a conceptual and methodological exploration', *Studies in the Education of Adults* 17(1): 19–32.

Brookfield, S. (1986) *Understanding and Facilitating Adult Learning*, San Francisco: Jossey-Bass.

Brookfield, S. (1987) *Developing Critical Thinkers*, San Francisco: Jossey-Bass.

Brookfield, S. (1991) 'On ideology, pillage, language and risk: critical thinking and the tensions of critical practice', *Studies in Continuing Education* 13(1): 1–14.

Brookfield, S. (1993a) 'Breaking the code: engaging practitioners in critical analysis of adult education literature', *Studies in the Education of Adults* 25: 64–91.

Brookfield, S. (1993b) 'Self-directed learning, political clarity, and the critical practice of adult education', *Adult Education Quarterly* 43(4): 227–42.

Brookfield, S. (1994) 'Tales from the dark side: a phenomenography of adult critical reflection', *International Journal of Lifelong Education* 13(3): 203–16.

Broughton, J. M. (1981a) 'Piaget's structural developmental psychology: Piaget and structuralism', *Human Development* 24: 78–109.

Broughton, J. M. (1981b) 'Piaget's structural developmental psychology: ideology-critique and the possibility of a critical developmental theory', *Human Development* 24: 382–411.

Bruner, J. (1966) *The Process of Education*, Cambridge, MA: Harvard University Press.

Bruner, J. (1971) *The Relevance of Education*, London: Allen & Unwin.

Bruner, J. (1990) *Acts of Meaning*, Cambridge, MA: Harvard University Press.

Buck-Morss, S. (1975) 'Socio-economic bias in Piaget's theory and its implications for cross-cultural studies', *Human Development* 18: 35–49.

Buehler, C. and Massarik, F. (eds) (1968) *The Course of Human Life*, New York: Springer.

Buss, A. R. (1979) 'Dialectics, history and development: the historical roots of the individual–society dialectic', in P.B. Baltes and O.G. Brim (eds) *Life-span Development and Behavior*, vol. 2, New York: Academic Press.

Caffarella, R. (1993) 'Self-directed learning', in S. Merriam (ed.) *An Update on Adult Learning Theory: New Directions in Adult and Continuing Education*, San Francisco: Jossey-Bass.

Caffarella, R. and Caffarella, E. (1986) 'Self-directedness and learning contracts in adult education', *Adult Education Quarterly* 36(4): 226–34.

Caffarella, R. and Olson, S. (1993) 'Psychosocial development of women', *Adult Education Quarterly* 43(3): 125–51.

Callahan, E. and McCluskey, K. (eds) (1983) *Lifespan Developmental Psychology: Non-normative Life Events*, New York: Academic Press.

Camus, A. (1995) *The First Man*, London: Hamish Hamilton.

Candy, P. (1991) *Self-direction for Lifelong Learning*, San Francisco: Jossey-Bass.

Carr, W. and Kemmis, S. (1983) *Becoming Critical: Knowing Through Action Research*, Waure Ponds: Deakin University Press.

Cartwright, D. and Zander, A. (1968) *Group Dynamics*, New York: Harper & Row.

Cattell, R. (1963) 'Theory of fluid and crystallized intelligence: a critical experiment', *Journal of Educational Psychology* 54(1): 1–22.

Chaiklin, S. and Lave, J. (eds) (1993) *Understanding Practice: Perspectives on Activity in Context*, Cambridge: Cambridge University Press.

Chi, M. T. H., Glaser, R. and Farr, M. J. (eds) (1988) *The Nature of Expertise*, Hillsdale, NJ: Lawrence Erlbaum.

Chickering, A. W. (1969) *Education and Identity*, San Francisco: Jossey-Bass.

Chickering, A. W. (1978) 'The double bind of field dependence/independence in program alternatives for educational development', in S. Messick and associates, *Individuality in Learning*, San Francisco: Jossey-Bass.

Chickering, A. W. (ed.) (1981) *The Modern American College*, San Francisco: Jossey-Bass.

Chickering, A. W. (1983) 'Education and work – and human development', *Journal of Continuing Higher Education* 31(2): 2–6.

Chickering, A. W. (1993) *Education and Identity,* San Francisco: Jossey-Bass.

Chickering, A. W. and Havighurst, R. (1981) 'The life cycle', in A.W. Chickering (ed.) *The Modern American College,* San Francisco: Jossey-Bass.

Chodorow, N. (1978) *The Reproduction of Mothering Psychoanalysis and the Sociology of Gender,* Berkeley, CA: University of California Press.

Chodorow, N. (1989) *Feminism and Psychoanalytic Theory,* New Haven, CT: Yale University Press.

Chomsky, N. (1959) Review of *Verbal Behavior* by B. F. Skinner, *Language* 35(1): 26–58.

Clark, M. C. and Wilson, A. L. (1991) 'Context and rationality in Mezirow's theory of transformational learning', *Adult Education Quarterly* 41(2): 75–91.

Colarusso, C. A. (1992) *Child and Adult Development: A Psychoanalytic Introduction for Clinicians,* New York: Plenum.

Colarusso, C. and Nemiroff, A. (1981) *Adult Development,* New York: Plenum.

Colby, A. and Kohlberg, L. (1987) *The Measurement of Moral Judgment,* vol. 2, *Standard Issue Scoring Manual,* Cambridge: Cambridge University Press.

Collins, M. (1991) *Adult Education as Vocation: A Critical Role for the Adult Educator,* London: Routledge.

Collins, M. (1995) 'The critical juncture: commitment, prospects, and the struggle for adult education in the academy', *Proceedings of the International Conference on Adult Education,* Canmore, Alberta, 15–17 May.

Connell, R. W. (1983) 'Dr Freud and the course of history', in R. W. Connell, *Which Way is Up? Essays on Class, Sex and Culture,* Sydney: Allen & Unwin.

Conti, G. (1985) 'The relationship between teaching style and adult student learning', *Adult Education Quarterly* 35(4): 220–8.

Conti, G. and Welborn, R. (1986) 'Teaching-learning styles and the adult learner', *Lifelong Learning* 9(8): 20–2.

Cooper, C. (ed.) (1975) *Theories of Group Processes,* London: Wiley.

Courtenay, B. (1994) 'Are psychological models of adult development still important for the practice of adult education?', *Adult Education Quarterly* 44(3): 145–53.

Cross, K. P. (1981) *Adults as Learners,* San Francisco: Jossey-Bass.

Danis, C. and Tremblay, N. (1987) 'Propositions regarding autodidactic learning and the implications for teaching', *Lifelong Learning: An Omnibus of Practice and Research* 10: 4–7.

Darkenwald, G. and Merriam, S. (1982) *Adult Education: Foundations of Practice,* New York: Harper & Row.

Datan, N. and Ginsberg, L. (eds) (1975) *Lifespan Developmental Psychology: Normative Life Crises,* New York: Academic Press.

Davies, B. (1989) *Frogs and Snails and Feminist Tales,* Sydney: Allen & Unwin.

Davis, R., Alexander, L. and Yelon, S. (1974) *Learning System Design,* New York: McGraw-Hill.

Dean, G. and Dowling, W. (1987) 'Community development: an adult education model', *Adult Education Quarterly* 37(2): 78–9.

Delahaye, B. L. and Smith, H. E. (1995) 'The validity of the learning preference assessment', *Adult Education Quarterly* 45(3): 159–73.

Delbecq, A., Van der Ven, A. and Gustafson, D. (1975) *Group Processes for Program Planning: A Guide to Nominal Group and Delphi Processes,* Glenview, IL: Scott Foreman.

Dixon, N. (1985) 'The implementation of learning style information', *Lifelong Learning* 9(3): 16–27.

Doise, W. (1978) *Groups and Individuals: Explanations in Social Psychology,* Cambridge: Cambridge University Press.

Doise, W., Mugny, G. and Perret-Clermont, A. (1976) 'Social interaction and cognitive development: further evidence', *European Journal of Social Psychology* 6(2): 245–7.

Douglas, T. (1989) *Groups,* London: Tavistock.

Dunphy, D. (1968) 'Phases, roles and myths in self-analytic groups', *Journal of Applied Behavioral Science* 4: 195–226.

Edwards, R. and Usher, R. (1995) 'Postmodernity and the educating of educators', *Proceedings of the International Conference on Adult Education,* Canmore, Alberta, 15–17 May.

Egan, K. (1984) *Education and Psychology,* London: Methuen.

Elkind, D. and Flavell, J. (eds) (1969) *Studies in Cognitive Development: Essays in Honor of Jean Piaget,* New York: Oxford University Press.

Entwhistle, N. (1981) *Styles of Learning and Teaching,* New York: Wiley.

Eraut, M. (1993) 'Implications for standards development', *Competence and Assessment* 21: 14–17.

Erikson, E. H. (1959) *Identity and the Life Cycle, Psychological Issues* I(1) (monograph no. 1).

Erikson, E. H. (1963) *Childhood and Society,* New York: Norton.

Erikson, E. H. (ed.) (1978) *Adulthood,* New York: Norton.

Feather, N. (1964) 'Acceptance and rejection of arguments in relation to attitude strength, critical ability and tolerance of inconsistency', *Journal of Abnormal and Social Psychology* 69(2): 127–36.

Field, L. (1989) 'An investigation into the structure, validity, and reliability of Guglielmino's self-directed learning scale', *Adult Education Quarterly* 39(3): 125–39.

Field, L. (1991) 'Guglielmino's self-directed learning readiness scale: should it continue to be used?', *Adult Education Quarterly* 41(2): 100–3.

Flavell, J. (1963) *The Developmental Psychology of Jean Piaget,* New York: Van Nostrand.

Flavell, J. (1971) 'Stage-related properties of cognitive development', *Cognitive Psychology* 2: 421–53.

Flavell, J. (1972) 'An analysis of cognitive developmental sequences', *Genetic Psychology Monographs* 86: 279–350.

Flavell, J. and Wohlwill, J. (1969) 'Formal and functional aspects of cognitive development', in D. Elkind and J. Flavell (eds) *Studies in Cognitive Development: Essays in Honor of Jean Piaget,* New York: Oxford University Press.

Floyd, A. (1976) *Cognitive Styles,* Milton Keynes: Open University Press.

Foley, G. (1992) 'Going deeper: teaching and group work in adult education', *Studies in the Education of Adults* 24(2): 143–61.

Forsyth, D. R. (1990) *Group Dynamics,* Pacific Grove, CA: Brooks/Cole.

Freire, P. (1972) *Pedagogy of the Oppressed,* Harmondsworth: Penguin.

Freire, P. (1974) *Education: The Practice of Freedom,* London: Writers and Readers.

Freire, P. (1985) *The Politics of Education: Culture, Power and Liberation,* London: Macmillan.

Freire, P. (1989) *Learning to Question: A Pedagogy of Liberation,* New York: Continuum.

Freud, S. (1949) *An Outline of Psychoanalysis,* New York: Norton.

Freud, S. (1953) 'Fragment of an analysis of a case of hysteria', in J. Strachey (ed.) *Standard Edition of the Complete Psychological Works of Sigmund Freud,* vol. 7, London: Hogarth.

Freud, S. (1958) 'A note on the unconscious in psychoanalysis', in J. Strachey (ed.)

Standard Edition of the Complete Psychological Works of Sigmund Freud, vol. 12, London: Hogarth.

Freud, S. (1963) *Civilization and its Discontents*, London: Hogarth.

Freud, S. (1973a) *Introductory Lectures on Psychoanalysis*, Harmondsworth: Penguin.

Freud, S. (1973b) *New Introductory Lectures on Psychoanalysis*, Harmondsworth: Penguin.

Fromm, E. (1973) *The Crisis of Psychoanalysis*, Harmondsworth: Penguin.

Furst, E. (1981) 'Bloom's taxonomy of educational objectives for the cognitive domain: philosophy and educational issues', *Review of Educational Research* 51(4): 441–53.

Gage, N. L. (1976) *The Psychology of Teaching Methods*, Chicago: NSSE (National Society for the Study of Education).

Garrison, D. (1992) 'Critical thinking and self-directed learning in adult education: an analysis of responsibility and control issues', *Adult Education Quarterly* 42(3): 136–48.

Gelpi, E. (1979) *A Future for Lifelong Education*, vols 1 and 2, Manchester: Manchester Monographs.

Gilligan, C. (1986) *In a Different Voice*, Cambridge, MA: Harvard University Press.

Gilligan, C. and Kohlberg, L. (1978) 'From adolescence to adulthood: the rediscovery of reality in a post-conventional world', in M. H. Appel, B. Z. Presseisen and P. Goldstein (eds) *Topics in Cognitive Development*, vol. 2, *Language and Operational Thought*, New York: Plenum.

Goldstein, K. (1939) *The Organism*, Boston, MA: Beacon.

Golembiewski, R. (1962) *The Small Group*, Chicago: Chicago University Press.

Gonczi, A. (1994) 'Competency based assessment in the professions in Australia', *Assessment in Education* 1(1): 24–36.

Gonczi, A., Hager, P. and Athanasou, J. (1993) *The Development of Competency Based Assessment Strategies for the Professions*, National Office of Overseas Skills Recognition Paper no. 1, Canberra: Department of Employment Education and Training.

Gore, J. M. (1993) *The Struggle for Pedagogies: Critical and Feminist Discourses as Regimes of Truth*, London: Routledge.

Goslin, D. A. (ed.) (1969) *Handbook of Socialization Theory and Research*, New York: Rand McNally.

Gould, R. (1972) 'The phases of adult life', *American Journal of Psychiatry* 129(5): 521–31.

Gould, R. (1978) *Transformations: Growth and Change in Adult Life*, New York: Simon & Schuster.

Gould, R. (1990) 'Clinical lessons from adult developmental theory', in R. Nemiroff and C. Colarusso (eds), *New Dimensions in Adult Development*, New York: Basic Books.

Goulet, L. R. and Baltes, P. B. (eds) (1970) *Lifespan Developmental Psychology*, New York: Academic Press.

Griffin, C. (1983) *Curriculum Theory in Adult and Lifelong Education*, London: Croom Helm.

Griffin, C. (1987) *Adult Education and Social Policy*, London: Croom Helm.

Gronlund, N. E. (1985) *Stating Behavioural Objectives for Classroom Instruction* (3rd edn), New York: Macmillan.

Gronlund, N. E. and Linn, R. L. (1990) *Measurement and Evaluation in Teaching*, New York: Macmillan.

Guglielmino, L. M. and Guglielmino, P. J. (1982) *Self-directed Learning Readiness Scale*, Boca Raton, FL: Guglielmino and Associates.

Guglielmino, P. J. and Guglielmino, L. M. (1991) *The Learning Preference Assessment*, USA: Organization Design and Development.

Guglielmino, L. M., Long, H. B. and McCune, S. K. (1989) 'Reactions to Field's investigation of the SDLRS', *Adult Education Quarterly* 39(4): 235–45.

Habermas, J. (1972) *Knowledge and Human Interests*, London: Heinemann.

Habermas, J. (1979) *Communication and the Evolution of Society*, Boston, MA: Beacon.

Habermas, J. (1984) *The Theory of Communicative Action*, Boston, MA: Beacon.

Hager, P. and Beckett, D. (1995) 'Philosophical underpinnings of the integrated conception of competence', *Educational Philosophy and Theory* 27(1): 1–24.

Hager, P. and Gonczi, A. (1993) 'Attributes and competence', *Australian and New Zealand Journal of Vocational Educational Research* 1(1): 36–45.

Hammond, M. and Collins, R. (1991) *Self-directed Learning*, London: Kogan Page.

Hare, P. (1976) *Handbook of Small Group Research*, London: Free Press.

Harré, R. (1974) 'Blueprint for a new science', in N. Armistead (ed.) *Reconstructing Social Psychology*, Harmondsworth: Penguin.

Hart, M. (1985) 'Thematization of power, the search for common interests and self reflections: towards a comprehensive theory of emancipatory education', *International Journal of Lifelong Education* 4(2): 119–34.

Hart, M. (1990a) 'Critical theory and beyond: future perspectives on emancipatory education and social action', *Adult Education Quarterly* 40(3): 125–38.

Hart, M. (1990b) 'Liberation through consciousness raising', in J. Mezirow (ed.) *Fostering Critical Reflection in Adulthood: A Guide to Transformative and Emancipatory Learning*, San Francisco: Jossey-Bass.

Hartree, A. (1984) 'Malcolm Knowles' theory of andragogy: a critique', *International Journal of Lifelong Education* 3(3): 203–10.

Havighurst, R. J. (1972) *Developmental Tasks and Education* (3rd edn), New York: McKay.

Hayes, E. (1989) 'Insights from women's experiences for teaching and learning', in E. Hayes (ed.) *Effective Teaching Styles: New Directions for Adult and Continuing Education*, San Francisco: Jossey-Bass.

Henry, R. M. (1980) 'A theoretical and empirical analysis of reasoning in the socialisation of young children', *Human Development* 23: 105–25.

Heron, J. (1975) *Six Category Intervention Analysis*, Human Potential Research project, Guildford: University of Surrey.

Hiemstra, R. and Sisco, B. (1990) *Individualising Instruction: Making Learning Personal, Powerful and Successful*, San Francisco: Jossey-Bass.

Horn, J. and Cattell, R. (1967) 'Age differences in fluid and crystallized intelligence', *Acta Psychologica* 26: 107–29.

Horn, J. and Cattell, R. (1968) 'Refinement and test of the theory of fluid and crystallized intelligence', *Journal of Educational Psychology* 57: 253–70.

Horton, M. (1986) Seminar held at the Aboriginal Training and Cultural Institute, Sydney, Australia.

Horton, M., Kohl, J. and Kohl, H. (1990) *The Long Haul: An Autobiography*, New York: Doubleday.

Houle, C. (1972) *The Design of Education*, San Francisco: Jossey-Bass.

Houle, C. O. (1992) *The Literature of Adult Education: A Bibliographic Essay*, San Francisco: Jossey-Bass.

Huberman, A. M. (1974) *Some Models of Adult Learning and Adult Change*, Strasbourg: Council of Europe.

Hughes, K. P. (1995) 'Feminist pedagogy and feminist epistemology: an overview', *International Journal of Lifelong Education* 14(3): 214–30.

Jacoby, R. (1975) *Social Amnesia*, Boston, MA: Beacon.

Jahoda, M. (1977) *Freud and the Dilemmas of Psychology*, London: Hogarth.

Jaques, D. (1992) *Learning in Groups* (2nd edn), Houston, TX: Gulf.

Jarvis, P. (1983) *Adult and Continuing Education: Theory and Practice*, London: Croom Helm.

Jarvis, P. (1984) 'Andragogy: a sign of the times', *Studies in the Education of Adults* 16: 32–8.

Jarvis, P. (1987a) *Adult Learning in the Social Context*, London: Croom Helm.

Jarvis, P. (1987b) 'Meaningful and meaningless experience: towards an analysis of learning from life', *Adult Education Quarterly* 37(3): 164–72.

Jarvis, P. (1992) *Paradoxes of Learning*, San Francisco: Jossey-Bass.

Kasworm, C. (1983) 'Self-directed learning and lifespan development', *International Journal of Lifelong Education* 2(1): 29–46.

Kaufman, A. S. (1990) *Assessing Adolescent and Adult Intelligence*, Boston, MA: Allyn & Bacon.

Keddie, N. 'Adult education: a women's service?', unpublished paper.

Kemmis, S. (1985) 'Action research and the politics of reflection', in D. Boud, R. Keogh and D. Walker (eds) *Reflection: Turning Experience into Learning*, London: Kogan Page.

Kemmis, S. and McTaggart, R. (1982) *The Action Research Planner*, Waure Ponds: Deakin University Press.

Kimmel, D. C. (1980) *Adulthood and Ageing*, New York: Wiley.

Kitchener, K. and King, P. (1994) *Developing Reflective Judgment*, San Francisco: Jossey-Bass.

Knowles, M. (1975) *Self-directed Learning*, New York: Association Press.

Knowles, M. (1980) *The Modern Practice of Adult Education* (2nd edn), Chicago: Association Press.

Knowles, M. (ed.) (1984) *Andragogy in Action*, San Francisco: Jossey-Bass.

Knowles, M. (1989) *The Making of an Adult Educator*, San Francisco: Jossey-Bass.

Knowles, M. (1990a) 'Fostering competence in self-directed learning', in R. M. Smith and associates, *Learning to Learn Across the Lifespan*, San Francisco: Jossey-Bass.

Knowles, M. (1990b) *The Adult Learner: A Neglected Species* (4th edn), Houston, TX: Gulf.

Knox, A. (1977) *Adult Development and Learning*, San Francisco: Jossey-Bass.

Knox, A. (1979) 'Research insights into adult learning', in T. Schuller and J. Megarry (eds) *Recurrent Education and Lifelong Learning*, London: Kogan.

Kohlberg, L. (1969) 'Stage and sequence: the cognitive-development approach to socialisation', in D.A. Goslin (ed.) *Handbook of Socialization Theory and Research*, New York: Rand McNally.

Kohlberg, L. (1971) 'From is to ought: how to commit the naturalistic fallacy and get away with it', in T. Mischel (ed.) *Cognitive Development and Epistemology*, New York: Academic Press.

Kohlberg, L. (1973) 'Moral judgement interview', unpublished manuscript, Harvard Graduate School of Education, Cambridge, MA.

Kohlberg, L. and Gilligan, C. (1971) 'The adolescent as a philosopher: the discovery of the self in a post-conventional world', *Daedalus* 100: 1,051–86.

Kolb, D. (1976) *The Learning Style Inventory: Technical Manual*, Boston, MA: McBer.

Kolb, D. (1981) 'Learning styles and disciplinary differences', in A. W. Chickering (ed.) *The Modern American College*, San Francisco: Jossey-Bass..

Kolb, D. (1984) *Experiential Learning*, Englewood Cliffs, NJ: Prentice-Hall.

Kolb, D. and Fry, R. (1975) 'Towards an applied theory of experiential learning', in C. Cooper (ed.) *Theories of Group Processes*, London: Wiley.

Kolb, D., Rubin, I. and McIntyre, J. (1984) *Organizational Psychology*, Englewood Cliffs, NJ: Prentice-Hall.

Kramer, D. (1986) 'A life-span view of social cognition', *Educational Gerontology* 12(4): 277–90.

Labouvie-Vief, G. (1977) 'Adult cognitive development: in search of alternative interpretations', *Merrill-Palmer Quarterly* 24(4).

Labouvie-Vief, G. (1980) 'Beyond formal operations: uses and limits of pure logic in lifespan development', *Human Development* 23: 141–61.

Labouvie-Vief, G. (1985) 'Intelligence and cognition', in J. E. Birren and K. W. Schaie (eds) *Handbook of the Psychology of Aging* (2nd edn), New York: Van Nostrand Reinhold.

Labouvie-Vief, G. (1990) 'Wisdom as integrated thought: historical and developmental perspectives', in R. J. Sternberg (ed.) *Wisdom: Its Nature, Origins, and Development*, Cambridge: Cambridge University Press.

Langer, E. J., Chanowitz, B., Palmerino, M., Jacobs, S., Rhodes, M. and Thayer, P. (1990) 'Nonsequential development and aging', in C. N. Alexander and E. J. Langer (eds) *Higher Stages of Human Development*, Oxford: Oxford University Press.

Lave, J. (1993) 'The practice of learning', in S. Chaiklin and J. Lave (eds) *Understanding Practice: Perspectives on Activity in Context*, Cambridge: Cambridge University Press.

Lave, J. and Wenger, E. (1991) *Situated Learning: Legitimate Peripheral Participation*, Cambridge: Cambridge University Press.

Lawson, K. (1975) *Philosophical Concepts and Values in Adult Education*, Nottingham: University of Nottingham.

Levinson, D. (1978) *The Seasons of a Man's Life*, New York: Knopf.

Levinson, D. (1986) 'A conception of adult development', *American Psychologist* 41: 3–13.

Levinson, D. (1990) 'The seasons of a woman's life: implications for men', Paper presented at the 98th Annual Convention of the American Psychological Association, Boston, MA.

Lewin, K. (1958) 'Group decision and social change', in E. Maccoby, M. Newcomb and E. Hartley (eds) *Readings in Social Psychology*, New York: Holt, Rinehart & Winston.

Loevinger, J. (1976) *Ego Development*, San Francisco: Jossey-Bass.

Loevinger, J. (1987) *Paradigms of Personality*, New York: Freeman.

Long, H. (1983) *Adult Learning: Research and Practice*, New York: Cambridge University Press.

Lovell, B. (1980) *Adult Learning*, London: Croom Helm.

Lovett, T. (1975) *Adult Education, Community Development and the Working Class*, London: Ward Lock.

Lovett, T., Clark, C. and Kilmurray, A. (1983) *Adult Education and Community Action*, London: Croom Helm.

Lowenthal, M., Thurnher, M. and Chiriboga, D. (1977) *Four Stages of Life*, San Francisco: Jossey-Bass.

Lukes, S. (1973) *Individualism*, Oxford: Basil Blackwell.

McCoy, V. (1977) 'Adult life cycle change: how does growth affect our education needs?', *Lifelong Learning: The Adult Years* 31: 14–18.

MacDonald-Ross, M. (1975) 'Behavioural objectives: a critical review', in L. Dobson, T. Gear and A. Westoby (eds) *Management in Education*, vol. 2, *Some Techniques and Systems*, London: Ward Lock.

McGurk, H. (ed.) (1978) *Issues in Childhood Social Development*, London: Methuen.

McLeish, J., Matheson, W. and Park, J. (1973) *The Psychology of the Learning Group*, London: Hutchinson.

Malcolm, A. (1975) *The Tyranny of the Group*, Totowa, NJ: Adams.

Mann, R. (1967) *Interpersonal Styles and Group Development*, New York: Wiley.

Marcuse, H. (1969) *Eros and Civilisation*, London: Sphere.

Martin, J. (1980) 'Perspectives on person and society', unpublished manuscript, Sydney: Macquarie University.

Maslow, A. (1968a) *Towards a Psychology of Being*, New York: Van Nostrand.

Maslow, A. (1968b) 'Some educational implications of the humanistic psychologies', *Harvard Educational Review* 36: 685–96.

Mead, G. H. (1972) *On Social Psychology*, selected papers edited by A. Strauss, Chicago: University of Chicago Press.

Melton, R. (1978) 'Resolution of conflicting claims concerning the effect of behavioural objectives on student learning', *Review of Educational Research* 48(2): 291–302.

Merriam, S. and Caffarella, R. (1991) *Learning in Adulthood*, San Francisco: Jossey-Bass.

Merriam, S. and Clark, M.C. (1991) *Lifelines: Patterns of Work, Love, and Learning in Adulthood*, San Francisco: Jossey-Bass.

Messick, S. and associates (1978) *Individuality in Learning*, San Francisco: Jossey-Bass.

Mezirow, J. (1983) 'A critical theory of adult learning and education', in M. Tight (ed.) *Adult Learning and Education*, London: Croom Helm.

Mezirow, J. (1985) 'A critical theory of self-directed learning', in S. Brookfield (ed.) *Self-directed Learning: From Theory to Practice*, San Francisco: Jossey-Bass.

Mezirow, J. (ed.) (1990) *Fostering Critical Reflection in Adulthood: A Guide to Transformative and Emancipatory Learning*, San Francisco: Jossey-Bass.

Mezirow, J. (1991a) *Transformative Dimensions of Adult Learning*, San Francisco: Jossey-Bass.

Mezirow, J. (1991b) 'Transformation theory and cultural context: a reply to Clark and Wilson', *Adult Education Quarterly* 41(3): 188–92.

Mezirow, J. (1992) 'Transformation theory: critique and confusion', *Adult Education Quarterly* 42(4): 250–2.

Mezirow, J. (1994) 'Understanding transformation theory', *Adult Education Quarterly* 44(4): 222–32.

Miles, M. (1955) 'Human relations training: how a group grows', *Teachers College Record* 55.

Milgram, S. (1965) 'Some conditions of obedience and disobedience to authority', *Human Relations* 18(1): 57–76.

Mills, T. (1964) *Group Transformation: An Analysis of a Learning Group*, Englewood Cliffs, NJ: Prentice-Hall.

Mischel, T. (ed.) (1971) *Cognitive Development and Epistemology*, New York: Academic Press.

Modgil, S. and Modgil, C. (1976) *Piagetian Research: Compilation and Commentary*, vol. 6, Windsor: National Foundation for Educational Research.

Modgil, S. and Modgil, C. (1986) *Lawrence Kohlberg: Consensus and Controversy*, London: Falmer.

Morelli, E. (1978) 'The sixth state of moral development', *Journal of Education* 7: 97–108.

Moreno, J. (1941) 'Foundations of sociometry: an introduction', *Sociometry* 4: 15–35.

Moreno, J. (1953) *Who Shall Survive?*, New York: Beacon.

Mugny, G. and Doise, W. (1978) 'Socio-cognitive conflict and structure of individual and collective performances', *European Journal of Social Psychology* 8: 181–92.

Musgrove, F. (1977) *Margins of the Mind*, London: Methuen.

Napier, R. and Gershenfeld, M. (1989) *Groups: Theory and Experience* (4th edn), Boston, MA: Houghton Mifflin.

Neugarten, B. L. (ed.) (1968) *Middle Age and Aging*, Chicago: University of Chicago Press.

New London Group (1996) 'A pedagogy of multiliteracies: designing social futures', *Higher Education Review* 66(1): 60–92.

Newman, M. (1979) *The Poor Cousin*, London: Allen & Unwin.

Newman, M. (1993) *The Third Contract: Theory and Practice in Trade Union Training*, Sydney: Stewart Victor.

Newman, M. (1994) *Defining the Enemy: Adult Education in Social Action*, Sydney: Stewart Victor.

Nottingham Andragogy Group (1983) *Towards a Developmental Theory of Andragogy*, Nottingham: University of Nottingham.

OECD (Organization for Economic Co-operation and Development) (1973) *Recurrent Education: A Strategy for Lifelong Learning*, Paris: CERI (Centre for Educational Research and Innovation).

OECD (1979) *Recurrent Education for the 1980s: Trends and Policies*, Paris: CERI.

Olmsted, M. and Hare, P. (1978) *The Small Group*, New York: Random House.

Pavlov, I. P. (1927) *Conditioned Reflexes*, trans. G. V. Anred, Oxford: Oxford University Press.

Perry, W. (1981) 'Cognitive and ethical growth: the making of meaning', in A. Chickering (ed.) *The Modern American College*, San Francisco: Jossey-Bass.

Peters, R. S. (1971) 'Moral development: a plea for pluralism', in T. Mischel (ed.) *Cognitive Development and Epistemology*, New York: Academic Press.

Piaget, J. (1954) *The Construction of Reality in the Child*, New York: Basic Books.

Piaget, J. (1955) 'Les stages du développment intellectuel de l'enfant et de l'adolescent', in P. Osterrieth *et al.*, *Le problème des études en psychologie de l'enfant*, Paris: Presses Universitaires de France.

Piaget, J. (1973) *The Child's Conception of the World*, London: Paladin.

Piaget, J. (1977a) *The Moral Judgement of the Child*, Harmondsworth: Penguin.

Piaget, J. (1977b) 'Problems of equilibration', in M. H. Appel and L. B. Goldberg (eds) *Topics in Cognitive Development*, vol. 1, *Equilibration: Theory Research and Application*, New York: Plenum.

Piaget, J. (1978) *The Development of Thought: Equilibration of Cognitive Structures*, Oxford: Basil Blackwell.

Piaget, J. and Inhelder, B. (1956) *The Child's Conception of Space*, London: Routledge & Kegan Paul.

Pietrykowski, B. (1996) 'Knowledge and power in adult education: beyond Freire and Habermas', *Adult Education Quarterly* 46(2): 82–97.

Podeschi, R. and Pearson, E. (1986) 'Knowles and Maslow: differences about freedom', *Lifelong Learning* 9(7): 16–18.

Pratt, D. (1993) 'Andragogy after twenty-five years', in S. Merriam (ed.) *An Update on Adult Learning: New Directions in Adult and Continuing Education*, San Francisco: Jossey-Bass.

Reese, H. and Overton, W. (1970) 'Models of development and theories of development', in L. R. Goulet and P. B. Baltes (eds) *Lifespan Developmental Psychology*, New York: Academic Press.

Reich, W. (1972) *The Sexual Revolution*, London: Vision Press.

Riegel, K. F. (1973) 'Dialectical operations: the final period of cognitive development', *Human Development* 16: 346–70.

Riegel, K. F. (1975) 'Adult life crises: a dialectical interpretation of development', in N. Datan and L. Ginsberg (eds) *Lifespan Developmental Psychology: Normative Life Crises*, New York: Academic Press.

Riegel, K. F. (1976) 'The dialectics of human development', *American Psychologist* October: 689–99.

Riegel, K. F. (1978) *Psychology Mon Amour: A Countertext*, Boston, MA: Houghton Mifflin.

Riegel, K. F. and Rosenwald, G. (eds) (1975) *Structure and Transformation*, New York: Wiley.

Roazen, P. (1976) *Erik H. Erikson*, New York: Free Press.

Robinson, J. and Taylor, D. (1983) 'Behavioural objectives in training for adult education', *International Journal of Lifelong Education* 2(4): 355–70.

Rogers, C. (1951) *Client-centred Therapy*, Boston, MA: Houghton Mifflin.

Rogers, C. (1983) *Freedom to Learn for the 1980s*, Columbus, OH: Merrill.

Rotman, B. (1977) *Jean Piaget: Psychologist of the Real*, Brighton: Harvester.

Rybash, J., Hoyer, W. and Roodin, P. (1986) *Adult Cognition and Aging*, New York: Pergamon.

Salzberger-Wittenberg, I., Henry, G. and Osborne, E. (1983) *The Emotional Experience of Learning and Teaching*, London: Routledge & Kegan Paul.

Scannell, E. and Newstrom, J. (1983) *More Games Trainers Play*, New York: McGraw-Hill.

Schaie, K. (1965) 'A general model for the study of development problems', *Psychological Bulletin* 64: 92–107.

Schaie, K. (1973) 'Methodological problems in descriptive developmental research on adulthood and aging', in J. Nesselroade and N. Reese (eds) *Lifespan Developmental Psychology: Methodological Issues*, New York: Academic Press.

Schaie, K. (1979) 'The primary mental abilities in adulthood: an exploration in the development of psychometric intelligence', in P.B. Baltes and O.G. Brim (eds) *Life-span Development and Behavior*, vol. 2, New York: Academic Press.

Schaie, K. W. (1983a) *Longitudinal Studies of Adult Psychological Development*, New York: Guilford.

Schaie, K. W. (1983b) 'The Seattle Longitudinal Study: a 21-year exploration of psychometric intelligence in adulthood', in K. W. Schaie (ed.) *Longitudinal Studies of Adult Psychological Development*, New York: Guilford.

Schaie, K. W. and Willis, S. (1986) 'Can adult intellectual decline be reversed?', *Developmental Psychology* 22: 223–32.

Schmidt, H. G., Norman, G. R. and Boshuizen, H. P. A. (1990) 'A cognitive perspective on medical expertise: theory and implications', *Academic Medicine* 65(10).

Schon, D. (1987) *Educating the Reflective Practitioner*, San Francisco: Jossey-Bass.

Schutz, W. C. (1955) 'What makes groups productive?', *Human Relations* 8: 429–65.

Scribner, S. (1986) 'Thinking in action: some characteristics of practical thought', in R. J. Sternberg and R.K. Wagner (eds) *Practical Intelligence: Nature and Origins of Competence in the Everyday World*, Cambridge: Cambridge University Press.

Shaw, M. (1981) *Group Dynamics*, New York: McGraw-Hill.

Sherif, M. (1935) *The Psychology of Social Norms*, New York: Harper.

Shor, I. (1980) *Critical Teaching in Everyday Life*, Boston, MA: South End Press.

Shrewsbury, C. (1987) 'What is feminist pedagogy?', *Women's Studies Quarterly* 15: 6–14.

Simpson, E. L. (1974) 'Moral development research: a case study of scientific-cultural bias', *Human Development* 17: 81–106.

Skinner, B. F. (1938) *The Behaviour of Organisms: An Experimental Analysis*, New York: Appleton-Century-Crofts.

Skinner, B. F. (1959) *Science and Human Behaviour*, New York: Macmillan.

Skinner, B. F. (1973) *Beyond Freedom and Dignity*, Harmondsworth: Penguin.

Smith, R. M. (1984) *Learning How to Learn*, Milton Keynes: Open University Press.

Spear, D. and Mocker, D. (1984) 'The organising circumstance: environmental determinants in self-directed learning', *Adult Education Quarterly* 35(1): 1–10.

Squires, G. (1981) *Cognitive Styles and Adult Learning*, Nottingham: University of Nottingham.

Stalker, J. (1996) 'Women and adult education', *Adult Education Quarterly* 46(2): 98–113.

Sternberg, R. J. (ed.) (1990a) *Wisdom: Its Nature, Origins, and Development*, Cambridge: Cambridge University Press.

Sternberg, R. J. (1990b) *Intelligence and Adult Learning*, Papers from a Symposium Sponsored by the Center for Adult Learning Research, Montana State University.

Sternberg, R. J. and Wagner, R. K. (eds) (1986) *Practical Intelligence: Nature and Origins of Competence in the Everyday World*, Cambridge: Cambridge University Press.

Stevens-Long, J. (1979) *Adult Life: Developmental Processes*, Palo Alto, CA: Mayfield.

Sullivan, E. V. (1977) 'A study of Kohlberg's structural theory of moral development: a critique of liberal social science ideology', *Human Development* 20: 352–76.

Tennant, M. (1985a) 'Training adult educators: a case study', *Forum of Education* 44(2): 10–20.

Tennant, M. (1985b) 'The concept of "need" in adult education', *Australian Journal of Adult Education* 25(2): 8–12.

Tennant, M. (1986) 'An evaluation of Knowles' theory of adult learning', *International Journal of Lifelong Education* 5(2): 113–22.

Tennant, M. (1991a) 'Expertise as a dimension of adult development: implications for adult education', *New Education* 13(1): 46–57.

Tennant, M. (1991b) 'Establishing an adult teaching–learning relationship', *Australian Journal of Adult Education* 31(1): 4–9.

Tennant, M. (1993) 'Perspective transformation and adult development', *Adult Education Quarterly* 44(1): 34–42.

Tennant, M. (1994) 'Response to understanding transformation theory', *Adult Education Quarterly* 44(4): 233–5.

Tennant, M. and Pogson, P. (1995) *Learning and Change in the Adult Years: A Developmental Perspective*, San Francisco: Jossey-Bass.

Thelen, H. and Dickerman, W. (1949) 'Stereotypes and the growth of groups', *Educational Leadership* 6: 309–99.

Thompson, J. (ed.) (1980) *Adult Education for a Change*, London: Hutchinson.

Thompson, J. (1983) *Learning Liberation: Women's Response to Men's Education*, London: Croom Helm.

Thompson, J. (1985) Untitled paper presented at an AAAE (Australian Association of Adult Education) Adult Education Seminar, March, Sydney.

Tight, M. (ed.) (1983) *Adult Learning and Education*, London: Croom Helm.

Tough, A. (1967) *Learning without a Teacher: A Study of Tasks and Assistance during Adult Self-teaching Projects*, Toronto: Ontario Institute for Studies in Education.

Tough, A. (1968) *Why Adults Learn: A Study of the Major Reasons for Beginning and Continuing a Learning Project*, Toronto: Ontario Institute for Studies in Education.

Tough, A. (1979) *The Adult's Learning Projects: A Fresh Approach to Theory and Practice in Adult Learning*, Toronto: Ontario Institute for Studies in Education.

Tough, A. (1982) *Intentional Changes*, Chicago: Follett.

Tough, A. (1983) 'Self-planned learning and major personal change', in M. Tight (ed.) *Adult Learning and Education*, London: Croom Helm.

Tucker, B. and Huerta, C. (1987) 'A study of developmental tasks as perceived by young adult Mexican-American females', *Lifelong Learning* 10(4): 4–7.

Tuckman, B. (1965) 'Developmental sequence in small groups', *Psychological Bulletin* 63: 384–99.

Tuckman, B. and Jensen, M. (1977) 'Stages of small group development', *Group and Organisational Studies* 2: 4.

UNESCO (1972) *Learning To Be: The World of Education Today and Tomorrow* (Faure Report), Paris: UNESCO.

UNESCO (1976) *Foundations of Lifelong Education*, Oxford: Pergamon.

Usher, R. (1986a) 'Adult students and their experience: developing a resource for learning', *Studies in the Education of Adults* 18(1): 24–34.

Usher, R. (1986b) 'The theory–practice problem and psychology as a foundation discipline in adult education', *Proceedings of the Sixteenth Annual Conference of SCUTREA*, University of Hull: 103–12.

Usher, R. (1989) 'Locating experience in language: towards a post structuralist theory of experience', *Adult Education Quarterly* 40(1): 23–32.

Usher, R. (1992) 'Experience in adult education: a post-modern critique', *Journal of Philosophy of Education* 26: 201–14.

Usher, R. (1993) 'Disciplining adults: re-examining the place of disciplines in adult education', *Studies in Continuing Education* 15.

Vaillant, G. (1977) *Adaptation to Life*, Boston, MA: Little, Brown.

Vaillant, G. and Vaillant, C. (1990) 'Natural history of male psychological health: a forty-five year study of predictors of successful aging at age 65', *American Journal of Psychiatry* 147: 31–7.

Wapner, S. (1978) 'Process and context in the conception of cognitive style', in S. Messick and associates, *Individuality in Learning*, San Francisco: Jossey-Bass.

Watson, J. B. (1913) 'Psychology as the behaviorist views it', *Psychological Review* 20: 158.

Weathersby, R. (1981) 'Ego development', in A. W. Chickering (ed.) *The Modern American College*, San Francisco: Jossey-Bass.

Welton, M. (1995) 'The disintegration of andragogy: the demise of adult education?', *Proceedings of the International Conference on Adult Education*, Canmore, Alberta, 15–17 May.

Williams, C. (1993) 'The politics of nurturant teaching', *Studies in Continuing Education* 15(1): 50–62.

Wiltshire, H. (1973) 'The concepts of learning and need in adult education', *Studies in Adult Education* 5(1): 26–30.

Witkin, H. (1950) 'Perception of the upright when the direction of the force acting on the body is changed', *Journal of Experimental Psychology* 40: 93–106.

Witkin, H. (1978) 'Cognitive style in academic performance and in teacher–student relations', in S. Messick and associates, *Individuality in Learning*, San Francisco: Jossey-Bass.

Witkin, H. and Goodenough, D. (1981) *Cognitive Styles, Essence and Origins: Field Dependence and Field Independence*, Psychological Issues, Monograph 51, New York: International Universities Press.

Witkin, H., Goodenough, D. and Karp, S. (1967) 'Stability of cognitive style from childhood to young adulthood', *Journal of Personality and Social Psychology* 7: 291–300.

Witkin, H., Moore, C., Goodenough, D. and Cox, P. (1977) 'Field-dependent and field-independent cognitive styles and their educational implications', *Review of Educational Research* 47(1): 1–64.

Wozniak, R. B. (1975) 'Dialecticism and structuralism: the philosophical foundation of Soviet psychology and Piagetian cognitive developmental theory', in K. F. Riegel and G. Rosenwald (eds) *Structure and Transformation*, New York: Wiley.

Wrong, D. (1961) 'The oversocialised conception of man in modern sociology', *American Sociological Review* 26(2): 183–93.

Youniss, T. (1978) 'The nature of social development: a conceptual discussion of cognition', in H. McGurk (ed.) *Issues in Childhood Social Development*, London: Methuen.

Zander, A. (1983) *Making Groups Effective*, San Francisco: Jossey-Bass.

Zander, A. (1990) *Effective Social Action by Community Groups*, San Francisco: Jossey-Bass.

Zeichner, K. and Liston, D. (1987) 'Teaching student teachers to reflect', *Harvard Educational Review* 57(1): 23–48.

Index